SUPERCHARGED SALES AND SELLING

Y'ALL AIN'T RIGHT:
Selling to Difficult and Irrational Buyers

BOB ROSSI

Supercharged Sales and Selling
Y'all Ain't Right: Selling to Difficult and Irrational Buyers
by Bob Rossi

Published by Bob Rossi
5550 Charlotte Hwy. Lancaster, S.C. 29720
www.bobrossi.co

Copyright copyright 2021 Bob Rossi
All rights reserved. No portion of this book may be reproduced in any form without permission from the publisher, except as permitted by U.S. copyright law.
For permissions contact: rossi1968@mindspring.com or 803-804-3066

Book design by Marko Markovic, 5mediadesign
Edited by Amy

ISBN: 9798536957417 (paperbook)
ISBN: 9788499338308 (hardcover)
ASIN: B09JTVW581 (kindle)

Printed in USA
1st edition

Dedication

I DEDICATE THIS BOOK TO MY *spectacular wife, Linda Rossi, without whom this book would not be possible. She's absolutely AMAZING! One of a kind! When asked, "Have you met Linda Rossi?" no one ever has had to think about their answer. She lights up a room and brings joy to everyone around her. Her vibrant personality and zest for life are my inspiration.*

My sincere appreciation for all of the hard work she put forth in correcting and rewriting the better portion of this book. She deserves all of the credit for painstakingly proofreading and correcting my extensive use of commas and my jibber jabber. She's responsible for compiling my menagerie of words into some semblance of order while contending with a special needs son and balancing her incredible workload!

I'd like to thank her for who she is and for helping me to be the best that I can be. All my love!

Table of Contents

Dedication iii

Acknowledgments. vii

Preface ix

Introduction. xi

Chapter 1 | Y'all Ain't Right. 1

Chapter 2 | The Customer Is Always Right!. 9

Chapter 3 | Strategic Empathy 15

Chapter 4 | Everyone's Money is Green 21

Chapter 5 | What Is Sales Psychology?. 25

Chapter 6 | Ask the Right Questions 29

Chapter 7 | Building Rapport. 33

Chapter 8 | Playing Devil's Advocate 37

Chapter 9 | Adapt. 41

Chapter 10 | Be Honest and Sincere. 45

Chapter 11 | Choosing the Right Product or Service to Sell. 47

Chapter 12 | Use Your Time Wisely 53

Chapter 13 | The Smokin' Sales Process. 59

Chapter 14	Sell Like You're a Natural-Born Salesperson 61
Chapter 15	Mindset. 65
Chapter 16	My Cheat Sheet: Quick Reference Techniques and Fast Responses 69
Chapter 17	How To Purchase Anything At The Lowest Price . . 93
Chapter 18	Asking for and Negotiating to Get the Order 97
Chapter 19	Close the Door 103
Chapter 20	The Door Won't Close All the Way 107
Chapter 21	You Thought You Had a Deal… The Client Is Still Riding The Fence 111
Chapter 22	How to Deal With Difficult Clients After a Sale . . 113
Chapter 23	Practice Problem Solving 119
Chapter 24	Provocative Marketing of Your Product or Service 123
Chapter 25	The Business of Being in Business 127
Chapter 26	Company Policy for Extending Credit 133

Finale 137

Y'all Ain't Right "Funnies". 141

About the Author | Why Should You Listen to Me? 145

LIVING LIFE 149

Acknowledgments

I'D LIKE TO GIVE THANKS to my wonderful and loving family. To my father, Robert Rossi, Sr., for being a strong role model and someone I have always looked up to. His strength of character and wisdom have enabled me to excel in everything I do.

To my amazing daughter, Heather, who has the soul of an angel. Her warmth and compassion for others are unprecedented. People are drawn to her. Heather is an accomplished actress and vocalist who has always made me proud. She's a shining star, both on and off the stage!

To my son, Robert Rossi III, who's inspired me to have compassion and respect for people with special needs. He's taught me to slow down, live simply, and focus on what matters most in life. He's given me patience I never thought I would have.

To my beloved mother, Margaret Elizabeth Rossi, who shaped the person I am today. She made me feel special. She always put her family first. She inspired me to work hard, be unique, and live life to the fullest while maintaining my integrity. She's my definition of the perfect mother.

Special thanks to Grandma and Grandpa McAuliffe and Rossi, Aunt Millie, Ernest and Carol Laird, Gramsie, Aunt Pat, Alan, Peter, Cody, Everly, Kiaz, Van, Sarah, Joe, and Patches!

I love you all. Thank you from the bottom of my heart!

To my friends, employees, and business associates, I am sincerely grateful for your support.

Preface

THE SUBTITLE, "Y'ALL AIN'T RIGHT," is a Southern figure of speech. I've found many Southern phrases like this to be keen insight into reality. Southerners, in jest, have created numerous sayings and slang terms that are quite poignant. This book's title is meant to make people ask, "What does the author mean by that?" First, it's meant to attract you to buy this book! I guess it worked. Second, it implies a double meaning. One meaning is that clients are actually wrong. Their belief or viewpoint is incorrect. The other more sarcastic inference is that clients are odd or irrational. We've all encountered people we assume or believe have something wrong with them. We believe that there is no way that a sane person could possibly think that way. And so…

Please remember the Serenity Prayer when dealing with clients.

> *"God, grant me the serenity to accept the things I cannot change, the courage to change the things I can, and the wisdom to know the difference"* (Reinhold Niebuhr, 1951). *Remembering this will open the door to success and wealth.*

Introduction

MOST PEOPLE AND BUSINESSES ARE selling some kind of product or service, so knowing how to handle everything from your initial client meeting to the closing table is beneficial to those in sales and business. In this book, I've included some clear and simple strategies for handling clients before, during, and after a sale. I've also added some tips for successfully handling general business situations.

I have focused on what I feel is key to one's enormous success. There are hundreds of thousands of business books; however, I wanted to provide a simple, straightforward "cheat sheet" that you could easily refer to from time to time. The following chapters contain "no fat" and all substance. I hope everyone can find at least one helpful tip to amassing prosperity that makes this book a worthwhile read. These tips are my personal experience in a successful life, sales, and in business. It's been a wild and eye-opening ride!! Enjoy!

Chapter 1

Y'all Ain't Right

In the South, we say, "Y'all ain't right!"

Y'ALL CRAZY! Y'ALL NUTS! Y'all can't be serious? Y'all's opinions are wack! Y'all don't really believe that, do ya? How can y'all possibly think that way? Commit the expression "Y'all ain't right" to memory. This one simple slang term is spot on. Truer words couldn't be spoken. Refer to the expression often when dealing with others.

Of course, I don't really mean that all people and clients aren't right. Obviously, we all feel that our way of thinking and our opinions are right. Naturally, we believe that anyone who thinks differently or has the opposite opinion must be wrong. How can anyone hold beliefs that are the polar opposite of our beliefs? Are these people crazy? What could they possibly be thinking? How could they come to the wrong conclusion on something so blatantly obvious? Why doesn't everyone feel the same way that I do? "Y'all ain't right." I'm right because I know everything. Matter of fact, I am almost never wrong.

Let's face it; we all feel this way deep down. Realizing that other people have different opinions, beliefs, and thoughts is crucial to your success in sales, business, and life. I'm suggesting taking a path of thought that will allow you to navigate around people you don't understand. Take the path that allows you to continue to move forward even though others may be standing in your way. Learn to live with them! You can sell to them and do business with them, even if they completely disagree with you! It's not as hard as it may sound. Empathize with them!

For example, a potential client believes he shouldn't commit to a five-year loan because he's heard that next year we may have a recession. I may say something like, "I hear what you're saying. Would your belief in a possible recession 12 months from now prevent you from making any medium- to long-term decisions about your business?" I may say, "It is certain that you should have our product, and how would that change if we did have a recession?" I would verbalize what he is thinking. I would address the possibility of a recession.

Notice that I am not agreeing or disagreeing with him. I am letting him know that I hear him. I will continue to ask questions that make him examine his beliefs. After all, nobody can predict a recession. Is it better to do nothing and make no decisions? Rather, it is prudent to take calculated risks. A good salesperson needs to take his client's concerns and fears head-on. Bring out the "demons," so to speak. You need to fight your client's demons in front of him.

Empathizing means that you respect his feelings, even if you do not agree with them. It's not unethical to empathize with anyone. You're not lying or lowering your standards. You're not agreeing with them. You don't have to convince them that they're wrong in order to coexist. It's not your job to fix them. That was their mama's job! It's not your responsibility to change their mind.

Your goal should be to find that common ground that enables you to provide a product or service the client needs. The client may not even know that they need it. It's your job to explain why they need do, even if they wholeheartedly believe they don't. You need to open their eyes. You don't need to convince them that you are right and they are wrong. You need to do business while not converting their religion, so to speak. Many people don't realize they need something until someone explains to them why they should have it. A good salesman's job is to enlighten the client. Show them how your product or service is vital to their success. It's almost magical to sell something to someone who initially felt they didn't need or want it.

Notice I am not advocating for you to change their whole mindset. I'm saying that you can navigate around their opposing beliefs and still do business with them. You simply focus on your product or service's benefits. You circumvent their wrongful beliefs, views, and opinions by demonstrating how your product offers greater value than their reason for not having it.

Another example may be to say, "How much money are you losing each day by not having our product?" You may say, "If you know the product will prevent you from losing money, how can you justify prolonging the inevitable purchase?" You are confronting the client's fears. You are inspiring him to think logically and focus on the numbers. After all, a client's fear may be based on a previous transaction or bad experience with another salesman. Their fears or skepticism may be unfounded. You, the salesman, may not agree at all. You may not understand their fears. However, the magic happens when you can do business with people with completely different opinions who still recognize the value of your product or service. In other words, your product or service supersedes their "wrongful" beliefs. Again, you are not trying to change their wrongful beliefs. You are not trying to make them see that you are right and they are wrong.

You understand that "Y'all ain't right" and can still sell them something.

The main point here is that you should be willing to do business with clients regardless of if you feel they are right. If a client is irrational or just plain wrong, it's your job to figure out a way to sell him something. Do not judge your clients. Keep your eye on the ball and sell to all of them. Imagine that half of your clients are Republicans and the other half are Democrats. If you are only willing to sell to Republicans because you feel that all Democrats are wrong or vice versa, you will lose half of your business.

So, how do you sell to irrational people? How do you sell to someone whose views are all wrong? It's simpler than you think. Keep reading, and I'll tell you how.

Be an "Equal Opportunity Seller." Sell to everyone regardless of "race, creed, or color." There's no room for prejudice in life or in sales. If your client's money is green, they qualify as a buyer. Please stop trying to convert your clients into people who fit your preferred mold. You're not going to convince a Democrat to become a Republican. Stop wasting your valuable time. It's not your job to convert your clients. You will live in a constant state of frustration while you try to convince all of your clients that you're right and they're wrong. They may simply be unreasonable. Don't reason with your clients, period. Just because you feel you are the voice of reason doesn't mean that you are. More importantly, your clients may not think that you are, and you're losing precious rapport with them. The faster you come to the realization that your clients often aren't right and that's OK, the faster you will sell and the more productive you will be.

Ever hear the expression, "That's just the way they are?" I've heard it said about relatives whose behavior is strange. Rather than try to convert or explain why they are that way, the phrase "That's just the way he or she is" simply begs you to accept the behavior because this is just who they are. Stop trying to convert your clients. Accept them for who they are and what they believe. This is the underlying message throughout this book. If you already fully understand this, you can stop reading now. Don't condemn behavior or beliefs. It is what it is.

All businesses should greet their clients with "How can we help you?" or "What can we do for you?" Sales are all about what you can do for the customer. They only care about what you can do for them or how your product will help them. Salespeople should focus on the words "HELP" and "YOU." You always want to help your client. Keep "you" in mind, and use it consistently when talking with your client. Try not to use "I" unless it is absolutely necessary.

A salesperson's core focus should be on how the product or service can benefit the client. Your primary concern is to demonstrate your product's value as it relates to helping your client. Your client either wants your product's benefits or needs it to eliminate a problem they have. Most clients buy faster when the product makes their problem or pain point go away. All of your marketing, advertising, and communication should center on how the product or service will help the client eliminate pain points and/or offer amazing benefits! For example, "Our product cures the common cold!"

You need to see things the way your client sees them. It may be hard, but if you want to sell, you'll have to get used to seeing things through their eyes. Notice I did not say that you must agree with your client. You will never agree with or understand each client. Similarly, not every client will agree with or understand you. The word "understand" implies agreement, right? Not in the case of sales. Understanding means that you see what they see. I'm not necessarily agreeing with a client, but I understand.

Have you ever heard the phrase, "You can't reason with an unreasonable person?" My interpretation of this is that one needs to recognize that some people are just plain unreasonable. If you want to work with them, you need to identify and classify them as being unreasonable. You obviously cannot reason with them, so how do you reach them or sell to them?

It's actually not as difficult as you may think. You need to be tolerant and patient and accept the fact that they are unreasonable. Acceptance is not agreement. I'm sure you've heard the expression, "We agree to disagree." I would encourage you to agree to disagree—without verbalizing that to your client. Clients do not want you to tell them you think they are wrong or that you do not agree with them. Think to yourself, "That is just the way he feels." Don't pass judgment, and don't correct them.

Did you know that most gang members and cult followers joined the gang or cult to feel understood and accepted by others? These feelings are so powerful. Say to your client, "I hear what you're saying."

Getting deeper into human psychology, I will tell you that the feeling of being misunderstood is even more painful. Do you remember the last time you were misunderstood by a colleague or customer service representative? People crave to be understood and deeply resent when they're not. People may feel betrayed or hurt. If you can demonstrate to your client that you understand them, you will build rapport rapidly. That, my friends, is the first step in a fabulous sale.

Think about how different Republicans and Democrats feel about most issues. How do two parties think so differently?

How in the world can 100+ people in Congress be almost equally divided on nearly every issue? Wouldn't it be nice if they all came to the same conclusion on issues? Take the current topic in the headlines: the wall between the U.S. and Mexico. How can two parties view this topic so completely differently? Certainly one party must be right. To resolve their differences, each party must be tolerant and respectful of the other. Realizing that they may never agree with each other, they do need to understand each other to move forward.

Similarly, you need to be <u>tolerant</u> and <u>respectful</u> of your client's views to do business with him. It's vital to demonstrate an understanding of other people's views and perspectives. Clients want to know that you hear what they're saying. They want to believe that you see what they see. Once the client feels that you know where he's coming from, they'll bond with you. Bonding is the gateway to trust. Trust is power!

To summarize thus far: Handle each client with deference. Stop trying to fix or cure them. You're not trying to solve world peace. Your sale is not a life-or-death matter. Your integrity is not being questioned. Your deal has nothing to do with ethics or your morality. It is not your duty to convince your client that you are right and he is wrong.

Keep your eye on the sale, and as painful as it is, verbally summarize that you see what they see. Show empathy by demonstrating to your client that you see what he sees. You must summarize how they feel, but you may not like it. Summarizing their point of view will create a bond between you and your client. For example, you may say, "Mr. Smith, you're thinking that you should wait to make a decision until your horoscope recommends it." You may say, "Mr. Smith, you believe our machine is exactly what you've been looking for, but you simply can't buy it because it's painted a color that you feel is bad luck." Once you summarize it and repeat it back to them, you've effectively demonstrated that you see what he sees and feels. You're demonstrating that you understand. This rapport moves the sale forward much more easily.

Again, you do not necessarily agree with your client; you more than likely do not believe they are correct. You may say something like, "I hear what you're saying," and offer various ways to move forward. Do not be combative with them or make it seem like their point of view is nuts. Rather, respectfully deflect and attempt to get them to find a solution that allows you to move forward. Keep nudging them in an effort to sway them in your direction. For example, you may say, "The color may or may not be bad luck. However, not having it will certainly be bad."

When all else fails, sometimes time, a commodity often overlooked, can be on your side. You may be able to use time to your advantage. When your deal is at a standstill, you can suggest meeting with your client in the near future. Say "when" that future time is—maybe the next day or week. "I will call you on Thursday at 9 am, and we can talk more about how this product can benefit you." You're implementing the tactic of allowing your client to "sleep on it." Try to stay in control of the deal and don't bring it to a head if it looks like you're losing him. Time can be a weapon that can salvage your deal.

Chapter 2

The Customer Is Always Right!

EVERYONE HAS HEARD THE TERM that "the customer is always right." Obviously, we know that this is not true. It's a customer service philosophy. We've all had instances where a customer is positively wrong. The "customer is always right" does not literally mean that a seller or service provider should agree with a client in every situation. I believe the term refers to a seller's mindset in dealing with clients. It means that a successful seller must consider the golden rule and "do unto others as you would want them to do to you."

Moreover, unless your customer "believes" you know where they're coming from, you may be at an impasse with a sale. For example, you go to a four-star hotel, and there are no towels in the room, and the sheets have not been changed. You go to the front desk and voice your dissatisfaction. They tell you to "relax" and that when they get around to it, they'll bring your towels and change the sheets. Obviously, you become very upset and feel that the hotel is fraudulently claiming to be a four-star hotel. More importantly, as the customer, you do not feel that anyone thinks you are "right" in being upset. You will never "buy" their services again, and you are completely deaf to anything more they say.

Let's flip this and see how you would react if the front desk had said, "Oh my goodness, you must be kidding. We are so sorry for this huge mistake. You must feel that we are not deserving of a four-star rating. What can we do to fix this to be sure you are 100% satisfied?" In this example, the front desk is acknowledging and empowering you, the customer, and is in complete agreement with you. They acknowledge that they see what you see, that you are "right." Obviously, you have every reason to be irate in this case, but they understand you, and you are willing to listen and talk with them.

However, what if you, as the customer, used foul language or threatened the front desk employees with violence? Would we still say that the customer is always right? I suggest that in this example, the customer is partially right.

As a professional, you must make every effort to try to see through the customer's eyes and put yourself in their shoes. You may think that you would have handled the problem completely differently than your customer did. You may think that foul language and threats are completely inappropriate.

Try to see the customer's point of view. What if I told you that the customer washed dishes for five years to save enough money to take his wife to a four-star hotel? What if you knew that the customer only had five days to live, and his last wish was to stay at a four-star hotel? Would you then understand and empathize with his behavior and emotions? My answer would be that you may not agree with his inappropriate behavior, but you can now see where he is coming from. You now have insight that sheds light on his irrational behavior. That doesn't mean you agree or believe he is right to make threats. It does, however, allow you to see his perspective. If you had knew his history and current situation, you would have an advantage when dealing with him.

Clients are only people—and not everyone will pass your litmus test on morality, integrity, or ethics. As a matter of fact, some people may be downright dishonest and untrustworthy. It's your job to uncover your client's flaws and use this information to your benefit. The more you know about your clients and their idiosyncrasies, the greater advantage you will have. You don't necessarily have to know who you are dealing with; you don't have to know your client's history or reputation. But the more you know about your client, the better your position is in the deal.

Remember to sell to all of them. Modify your strategy accordingly to ensure you are most effective in dealing with a particular client type. You may even modify your strategy to cater to a client who is inherently mean or pessimistic. The point is to do what you have to do to stack the cards in your favor. Use mind games and tactics that give you the edge and upper hand.

Voss, a well-known FBI hostage negotiator, would say to repeat back to the client exactly what he sees and feels. You would tell the client, "You must be so disappointed after working so hard and saving for so long for this trip," or "You must be so disappointed that this isn't the premier four-star hotel experience you've been dreaming of." Again, this does not mean that you agree with the irrational behavior. It means that you empathize with the client and are looking to get to a mutual "that's right."

How does this apply to sales and the mantra "the customer is always right"? Very simply, clients and buyers can be irrational, and you must try to reiterate and convey that you "see what they see." You must break down the wall of irrationality by letting the proverbial "elephant in the room" out. If you have any chance of reaching the client, preserving a relationship, or getting the client to be even remotely satisfied, recite scripture and verse about what you think they are seeing and feeling and why. It's not going to be easy when you staunchly disagree. However, your goal is to sell your product and service and to use whatever "samurai" tactics you have to in order to achieve your goal.

Notice I am not talking about lying or sacrificing your ethics. I am not talking about lowering your standards or changing your religion. I am talking about using the tools in your arsenal to get the job done. If you want to take an ethical stand and try to convince the client or buyer that they are wrong, you will lose your rapport, your relationship with the client, and, most likely and more importantly, the deal. If you feel the client's behavior is so outrageous or contradictory to everything you stand for, you can be the judge if you want to continue to do business with them. My point is that if your focus is success in customer relations and sales, and the client hasn't hurt anyone, you should do what is necessary to sell your product or service while preserving your ethics.

Remember, "the client is always right," unless he is breaking the law. You don't have to agree to sell and keep the relationship alive. How many Democrats continue to negotiate with Republicans even though they staunchly disagree with each other? Are the politicians hypocrites, unholy, or unethical because they continue to talk with their counterparts? I would argue that it is OK to agree to disagree in most cases. Remember, the goal is to work towards a deal and/or common ground. Whether it be politics, sales, or service, you don't have to agree to get something accomplished.

You don't have to agree with the literal usage of the "customer is always right." You need to understand what the underlying message is in the phrase. I believe the author of "the customer is always right" was conveying the message that people need to be patient and tolerant of others even though they may not agree. If this tolerance leads to enriching the wallet of the tolerant, then one must be the judge of what is ethically "right" and "wrong."

In summation, I believe that what's meant by the term "the client is always right" is that we should recognize the client's position of power. As humans, we all want recognition for our accomplishments; we want to feel that we are in control of our lives. As a consumer, we have power. We have the power to buy or not buy. We have the power to help a salesperson meet their monthly quota. We have the power to buy stuff that, in turn, helps make others more profit. When we enter a restaurant, we are normally greeted and welcomed. A proper establishment will make us feel comfortable and cared for while recognizing that we are a patron with power. You don't have to go overboard and kiss the ground the buyer walks on, but you do need to show the buyer the respect they deserve.

We crave recognition. Even the greatest athlete who has been applauded by thousands over the years will expect applause and crave it after demonstrating greatness in the field. Movie stars and stage performers are no different. We are all human. We all want to be recognized. In its most basic form, serving customers means we recognize their power as buyers by showing them respect and recognition. You are demonstrating you appreciate them for frequenting your establishment, buying your goods, or using your services. I can assure you the buyer expects to be treated with admiration and respect. Think of it as your applause for a performer.

"The customer is always right" is more than its literal meaning. The term defines a seller's mindset towards a buyer. Show clients that you care about them and that you want to help them. Show clients that you acknowledge their power position in the figurative "driver's seat" as the buyer. This mindset is vital to your achieving success in business and in sales! Remember, sales and business is a percentages game. You are not going to win them all. You are not going to sell your product or service to every client. You will increase your chances and increase your percentage of sales, however, by adhering to the mantra that the "customer is always right" (within reason).

Chapter 3

Strategic Empathy

I'm going to give you one of the most powerful influence techniques. Strategic empathy is so empowering that it deserves its own chapter. This one technique is so powerful that it can be used for both good and evil. It should NOT be confused with "sympathy." Sympathy means that you feel sorry or pity for another person. Sympathy is the feeling that you agree with and understand the beliefs and feelings of someone from your own perspective.

Empathy is similar but with a twist. This "twist" is the key to success. Empathy means that you hear what the other person says and acknowledge their pain or feelings while putting yourself in their shoes. You may understand how a person feels the way he does based on his background or circumstances. Empathy does NOT mean that you agree with someone. You simply have a general understanding of their viewpoint and feelings. Empathy means you see what they see from their own perspective.

There is no greater sales power than identifying with your buyer. If you can effectively put yourself in the buyer's shoes and discuss the good and the bad, the buyer will feel more confident about their decision.

"I hear ya!" is an extremely powerful statement to use with a client. To agree and form a general bond with your client, you can use what I call strategic empathy. You use strategic empathy when you summarize your client's concerns or feelings. Again, it doesn't matter if you agree with his concerns or feelings. What matters is that your client believes that you see how he feels. Remember, you're not lying to the client. You are strategically attempting to develop trust. It will be much easier for the client to trust you if he believes that you "get" where he is coming from. Gang and cult leaders are experts at creating this type of trust-based influence. If it is powerful enough to convert people to join a gang or cult, imagine how it can help in sales!

Carl Rogers, a well-known psychologist, coined the phrase "cognitive empathy" in the 1970s. His research showed that cognitive empathy is the fastest and most effective way to develop trust. This type of empathy is often utilized by sociopaths to develop trust and persuade people to do nearly anything—a prime example of using empathy for evil. They focus on tactics like cognitive empathy to bend the reality of those they are trying to manipulate. Because the technique is so powerful and effective, lazy sociopaths become experts at implementing this system.

I am not suggesting that I admire sociopaths. I'm just demonstrating the power of empathy in getting people to do nearly anything. Please do not misuse these psychological "samurai" tactics for evil. Your goal is to sell ethically and to provide a product or service that will benefit your client. The psychological tactics we're using are an "expressway" for the sales process. Since time is a valuable commodity, why not jump on the expressway?

Using strategic empathy to close sales and to convince people is clean, fast, and very effective! Imagine, for example, that a family walks into a car dealership in desperate need of a new car. The salesman introduces himself and asks, "What brought you into the dealership today?" The family explains that their current vehicle is old and unreliable and that they had a horrible experience the last time they bought a new car. They paid too much, and the new car dealer would not honor any warranty claims whenever they had problems. They finally sold their new car and bought a used one. They tell the salesman that they've been limping by and spending thousands in repairs to keep the old car running. They need reliable transportation. If they are late to work one more time due to car trouble, they could be fired. Lastly, they tell the salesman that they don't know what to do. Maybe they'll just keep fixing their old car.

Now, I know what most of you are thinking. It seems like the family is damned if they do and damned if they don't. After all, if they're going to have problems, they may as well keep the old car—at least they don't have a large new car payment each month. You need to be careful you are not sympathizing with the family. You need to empathize, not sympathize.

How could you use strategic empathy in this situation? The salesman could say, "I hear what you're saying, but would one bad new car buying experience prevent you from ever buying a new car? Possibly the dealer you bought it from was the problem? Possibly the car you bought was a 'lemon?' There are millions of satisfied new car owners with reliable transportation!" The salesman is verbalizing that he sees what they see. He's relating to what they are saying based on their previous bad experience.

The redirect is that the salesman does not agree with them but offers them a solution that will solve their problem. He assures them that although they have had a bad experience in the past, his new car will be a savior for them. He provides references and shows testimonials on his website of incredibly satisfied new car owners. He has effectively communicated that he understands where they are coming from but offers a solution that makes the most sense moving forward. He does not sympathize and say, "Well, you've had some tough breaks, so I guess you should stick with your old car." He tells them that one bad experience should not prevent them from enjoying the massive benefits of reliability and technology that his new car offers. He offers assurances to satisfy the family's skepticism. He uses "strategic empathy" to see what they see while providing a solution and selling them the new car that will eliminate their problem. If the same salesman were sympathetic instead of empathetic, he would have sold nothing, and the family would continue to complain about their old, broken-down car.

Strategic empathy can be used just about everywhere. Regardless of ethnicity, religion, and gender, strategic empathy is an enormously powerful sales tool. It is a psychological tactic that cuts through and focuses on the real issue. Everyone wants others to see what they see. As humans, we trust and provide information to people we feel are similar to us. We bond with people who either agree with us or verbalize that they see where we are coming from. In sales, strategic empathy can save countless hours of pitching because clients will normally divulge their true concerns once they believe they can trust you and that you see what they see. Strategic empathy works on anyone that is closeable, but use it with integrity.

Sell like you're the buyer. What the heck does that mean? It means to put yourself, the salesman, in the buyer's shoes. We've already covered strategic empathy. Try to relate to the buyer and understand his perspective. The more you can relate to your buyer and empathize with him, the quicker you will build rapport and close a sale. You can take the fast lane to closing a sale if you sell like you're the buyer. And doesn't everyone want to take the fast lane?

Chapter 4

Everyone's Money is Green

A GREAT SALESPERSON CAN SELL TO anyone! Don't try to pick a particular type of client and only work with them. Be willing to work with anybody who qualifies or can benefit from your product or service. I've heard salespeople say that "this client is too hard to work with, and I will not pursue him." Do not adopt this attitude! Often, I believe we get clients "by default," meaning that nobody else will work with them. That is OK. You win when you sell. Why not sell to anyone and everyone?

I realize that your time is valuable. I am all about proper time management. You should allocate the appropriate amount of time to deal with a difficult client, but you should be able to handle them all. How can you do this?

Of course, some sales are just easy. The simpler or less expensive the product is, the less you need to understand the buyer's psychology. The buyer knows exactly what he wants and is ready to buy. In this case, don't overcomplicate things. Salespeople should always sell with ethics, don't waste time with a lengthy question-and-answer dialogue when the buyer is ready to buy. If you're curious, you can always ask the buyer why he is so sure. However, it is not necessary to understand the buyer's motivation unless you feel an obligation to tell him he is making a mistake. Know when to shut up and take the order. If the buyer asks, "How can I take delivery?" or "What are your payment terms?" stop conducting psychological research and close the deal.

In cards, the expression is "know when to fold 'em." Remember, it's OK to stop talking once the buyer has made up his mind to buy. If your procedure includes steps 1–7, it's OK to stop at step 3 or skip 4 and 5 and go right to close. You're not a robot. The sales procedure is a guideline, not a rulebook. If you're sure the game is over, why prolong it?

But what about the difficult client? To be a great salesperson, you need to understand that all buyers are not the same, even if your product may be the perfect solution for every buyer. You may believe that you have a one-size-fits-all product. However, the buyer is still not convinced and won't buy. What should you do to close the deal? Be patient and try to get into the far corners of the buyer's mind. Understanding their background, perspective, past experiences, relationships, religion, and more will enable you to better serve the buyer and make your product more personalized to him.

How your product relates to the buyer can be vital. You need to be sure the buyer feels certain by answering all of his questions and demonstrating that your product fulfills all of his needs. Obviously, you need to know what those needs are, so ask them. You can then relate your product or service to his personal requirements. Your job is to have an answer to all of his questions.

Make a list of questions your buyer should be able to answer as it relates to your product or service for sale. Make mental and written notes that will enable you to apply your product to the buyer's needs, and try to respond to each answer to your questions. You're trying to get into his head. You're going to use the buyer's answers to your questions to justify the sale, so listen carefully to what he says. You're mounting an army to attack the buyer's objections. The buyer is going to tell you his weaknesses, wants, and desires, giving you everything you need to sell him. No one can argue or dispute his own responses. If they do, they're saying that they are wrong.

By the way, never stop asking questions or gathering information until the sale is final. Your army of responses is now ready for battle. The more answers you get from buyers, the bigger and stronger your army will be. You don't want to be surprised halfway through battle. If you try to close prematurely or skip steps, you must be certain that you know the buyer is ready to buy. A great salesman may be able to recover from a premature close; however, it takes skill and old-fashioned salesmanship.

Following a more methodical path will not only raise the likelihood of a close but will also provide a higher percentage of closings. Selling is the science of percentages. You can calculate the percentage of clients who will buy every week or month. If you are closing 30% of your clients, you should try to get more clients to increase sales. The science is that it is better to have 100 clients rather than 10. If you close 30%, you will increase sales from 3 to 30 simply by having a larger funnel. Obviously, you should work on increasing your percentage or closing rate, but if you can't increase your rate, try increasing the total number of prospective clients. Either way, it is vital to understand that you will not close everyone no matter how hard you try. There will always be clients that you lead to water but don't take a drink. But after reading this book, hopefully they will be few and far between.

Don't be afraid to lose a few deals while pushing the envelope. You will win in the end. You're always learning and gaining valuable experience each and every time you lose a deal. Lose a deal on your terms. Nobody likes to strike out standing still. If you swing at a pitch, you have a shot at hitting it. Try different sales <u>pitches</u> to see what you can <u>hit</u> out of the park! Win some, lose some—at least you went down swinging.

Chapter 5

What Is Sales Psychology?

SALES PSYCHOLOGY IS ALL ABOUT understanding why the buyer wants what they want. It's about getting the buyer to explain where they're coming from and uncovering their true motivation. Experienced salespeople don't just blurt out their product's list of features. Experienced salespeople ask questions.

To understand the psychology of the buyer, you need to ask questions. The answers you receive are like gold—they have significant value. After all, you are trying to uncover the real reasons a buyer is considering a product by getting into their mind. If you're patient, they will tell you exactly why they feel a certain way and which experiences influence their decisions. The buyer will give you everything you need to understand him and sell him something. I can't stress enough that the sale is about the buyer and his needs! If you're having problems getting the buyer to open up, several psychological tactics have been proven to work.

Try "mirroring" your client. An example of mirroring would be to repeat the last 3–5 words a client has said. If the client says, "I really am interested, but I never make a decision without speaking to my wife," you should say, "Without speaking to your wife?" in an inquisitive tone. The client will likely elaborate. He may say, "Yeah, she is always the voice of reason. She doesn't like to rush into anything." You would then say, "Rush into anything?" Get the idea? The client keeps elaborating and giving you valuable insight into why he is not moving forward. Mirroring is a tactical, psychological tool that is rarely detected by a client. It is a "samurai" skill that uncovers all of the hidden objections and deep-seated concerns your client may have.

I've also used future pacing as a psychological tactic to try to plant a seed in my client's mind. I may say, "When you get your 'machine,' you'll never have to pay exorbitant fees to the state again." I am trying to get my client to see into the future. I want him to start to imagine what it will be like to be the owner of my product or user of my service. In addition, I added that his "losses" might go away. Notice I did not talk about the benefit of future ownership. I did a double whammy by incorporating future pacing with the client's fear of loss. The impact doubles when used correctly.

You should go on and on like a good preacher. You need to inspire your client and reinforce that what he is doing will benefit him. Most clients need to be motivated by the seller to quit procrastinating. A realtor should walk into the home they are showing and say to the prospective buyer, "Wow, this is exactly what you have been looking for!" The client will either agree immediately or tell the realtor why they do not like it. Either way, the realtor has gotten valuable information that will enable them to either sell this particular home or find another.

Basic human interaction and agreement consist of very little communication. A client can be motivated and enthused if a seller simply says, "This is impressive." Buyers are looking for your approval and agreement. Be honest, but use engaging and enthusiastic adjectives and adverbs to describe your product or service. Don't be a bump on a log during a presentation. Show some enthusiasm; it is contagious. You should be saying, "This is tremendous," or "The benefits to your company will be incredible," or "Can you imagine letting someone else have this product or service?" Appeal to their sense of loss to trigger a reaction.

Remember that we all share basic emotions. Everyone wants a certain amount of approval from others. People want to know that other people like or agree with them. Remember when you showed your parents a project you were proud of as a child? Your basic desire to get your parent's approval or praise was your driving force. A buyer may want the approval or praise of a colleague or you, the salesperson, when making a decision or choosing a product. Yes, most Type A businesspeople will say that they do not require anyone's approval when making a decision. This may be true, but I'm banking on the odds that most people will be encouraged and inspired when they receive praise, recognition, or approval from a valued source.

If you take away only one thing from this entire book, remember that your customers have the same basic needs and desires as you. Always put yourself in their shoes. Again, this does not mean that you must agree or understand their perspective. Empathy requires that we know where they are coming from, but we don't have to agree with where they are coming from.

A skilled salesperson will be able to recite verse and chapter the reasons a customer feels the way they do. The salesperson should say something to the buyer like, "You're hesitating to make a commitment because you were burned in the past." Or you may say, "The last time you spent money on a three-day seminar, you were really disappointed." You are demonstrating that you see what they see. You are not agreeing with the buyer but rather creating a bond that allows the buyer to think that you "get him."

More than likely, you will invoke a "that's right!" response from the buyer. While being interviewed on The Salesman Podcast, Voss says that getting to "that's right" is an aha moment—a crucial turning point when you actually bond with your client. It means you are both on the same page and your buyer feels connected to you. Until you establish this kind of bond, it will be difficult to sell your product or service. That's not to say that it is impossible. Focus on what works in most scenarios. Don't be afraid to make an incorrect statement to a buyer or client. If you are wrong, the client will correct you, and you will learn something, which may help you close a deal.

Becoming a sales savant requires you to use various weapons from your arsenal of sales tactics and implement them accordingly for a win. There is rarely a perfect sales process. However, there are some really good ones that will make you proud when done right. Having knowledge of human behavior and psychology and acknowledging that the buyer is first a human will enable you to make a more effective connection with him, which can only help your deal.

Chapter 6

Ask the Right Questions

Ask any question that will help you to identify why the buyer should have your product. You never know when you'll uncover something that may help or hurt your sale. For example, after five minutes of questions and answers, you find out the guy you're talking with can't buy anything until his divorce is final. This information can radically change how you approach this sale. You may ask when his divorce will be final. If it is six months away, you may want to ask when you should contact him again as he's likely conducting research for a possible purchase later.

However, there are plenty of clients who are ready to buy now. Your experiences in selling your product will help you create a list of questions to clinch the sale. As a professional salesperson, you can't ask too many questions. The questions should aim at steering the client toward your product or service. Clients love to talk about themselves. They feel like you care about them when you ask questions. In addition, you are demonstrating that you want to be sure your product or service is the "perfect fit" for them. The client's answers will actually help you close him.

Think of the way a doctor examines and questions you during an examination. The doctor has a series of questions targeted at uncovering any issue you may have. If your doctor doesn't ask questions, you might feel he has not conducted a thorough examination. You appreciate being questioned because it demonstrates that the doctor not only cares about you but also knows what he is doing. It's the same in sales. Salespeople should consider their questions as conducting research about a client.

It is important to ask one question that may provide multiple answers. What does this mean? If you were selling cars, for example, you might ask, "If we have that model in blue, are you planning to lease or buy?" This is a "close" but also lets you know how they plan to pay, if they are ready to buy your car now, and their preferred color. Any response from the client, including "I'm not ready," uncovers valuable information you can use to close them.

Sometimes, I ask questions that I know are misleading to uncover more information from a prospect. If you know the client cannot pay cash, you might respectfully ask, "Did you say you were paying cash if we have it in stock?" Wow, this will uncover their payment preference and readiness to purchase.

Remember, all of your questions should be targeted at not only closing but also at finding the main objection for them not to buy. There is normally one objection preventing the client from saying "yes." It may be unspoken. The client may not wish to share her real reason for not buying. It could be that they don't trust you yet. Keep asking questions until the client either closes or tells you 1–2 core objections they have. This process is like peeling an onion. Sometimes, you can't cut corners—you have to peel one layer at a time. Each layer may uncover another objection or concern that allows you to continue to ask questions. Like completing a maze, one door may open and funnel you in a different direction.

In sales, you continue to follow the path laid out by the answers to your questions. The client will tell you what you need to know to close him. Do you get it? The questions you ask should be specifically designed to force the client to divulge everything you need to sell them your product or service.

Most buyers are smarter than you think. They won't tell you all of their fears, either. Everyone has hidden thoughts and concerns that they don't want to share with others. Experienced salespeople can find ways to bring them out, address them, and close.

The sequence in which you ask the questions can help you get to the root of the matter quickly. You may ask, "Why are you looking at our product?" or "What other options do you have?" Don't be afraid of getting into the "meat" of the deal. Most buyers will respect your candor and directness. Being direct can be a sign that you are a straight shooter—after all, nobody wants to listen to a "salesman." Buyers want to give answers to people who want to help them. Build rapport by being direct and showing that you understand and care. The client can always tell you they are not prepared to share something with you. They just gave up something with that answer. You now know they are sensitive to a topic or particular question. You've peeled back another onion layer.

Chapter 7

Building Rapport

YOU ARE MORE LIKELY TO sell your product to a buyer who likes you and can relate to you. Buyers who feel you understand where they are coming from will want to divulge their innermost concerns. This does not mean you should be phony or make them think that you are their friend for life. However, it is OK to explain that many of your best clients felt the same way prior to buying your product. It is OK to say that you hear what they are saying. It is vital to empathize with your client.

Building rapport is much easier when the buyer believes you are an authority on your product. You need to show you are an expert on the product or industry. This makes you more believable to a buyer. Buyers love to discuss their situation with anyone they feel can relate through actual experience. Your rapport level can go from one to 10 by simply explaining that you've been in the same situation as the buyer.

Don't try to be the buyer's beer buddy. It's OK to shoot the sh*t with a buyer for a short amount of time, but do not cross the line. The buyer wants to know that you are an authority because he is relying on you. Maintaining rapport with the buyer requires that the buyer continues to believe that you are ethical, honest, and knowledgeable. Being funny or sharing similar interests is a very small part of your rapport building.

Stay away from discussions of politics, religion, or marriage. One wrong word could trigger a negative reaction from the buyer and cost you the rapport you have gained. Stick to your product and the client's financial concerns, and be serious enough to stay on target. Stay focused on the sale. Don't waste time talking about the weather. Act like your time is limited, and the client will respect your time. Act like you have all the time in the world, and the client will think he is your ONLY client!

If you tell your buyer you strongly disagree or that they are wrong, you will destroy your rapport and most likely jeopardize the sale. You are trying to coax your client into buying your product by using logic and your relationship. If your questions have been answered, you can use logical explanations to try to persuade your client to change his mind.

Continue to build rapport throughout the process. You don't want to be on the defensive. Keep asking questions that will eventually spark a "that's right" from your client. Some clients will require significantly more time than others. Your job is to uncover the one or two things the buyer can relate to that may influence their decision.

We've all heard someone say that their mind is made up and they're not purchasing. A great salesman will continue to ask questions. He'll continue to push and pry. He'll continue to loop back until the buyer refuses to talk anymore. I'm not advocating that you be a pest. You have to judge how far to push your client. As long as the client/buyer continues to communicate, keep going. You will probably uncover an inconsistency in their thinking that will enable you to continue the sales process. Be persistent and understand you're obligated to pursue the buyer. Treat your sale as a quest to help the buyer. You've already established rapport; now it's time to see how far your rapport will take you. It is rare to have a buyer that you've established rapport with become distant or mad at you.

Lastly, great salespeople know when they have enough rapport and have provided enough information to the client to ask the hard questions. Closing may require the salesperson to play "devil's advocate."

Chapter 8

Playing Devil's Advocate

IF YOU KNOW THE CLIENT needs and should have your product, you need to present everything they may be thinking about. This may mean that you divulge information harmful to your close. You may ask, "Why would I do that?" Because if you feel the client is conducting research before they buy your product, you should divulge it and debunk any myths or rumors before they find them. You don't want the client to be surprised by uncovering something they feel you should have mentioned.

Tell them your product or service may be more expensive, then explain why. Tell them they may find another brand with a longer warranty, then explain why yours doesn't require one. By providing answers upfront, your deal will be more solidified, and your client will be more trusting. Remember, once your client walks away from your meeting, he is among the wolves—your competition. You need to prepare them for the answers your competition will feed him.

A good politician never waits to be asked the tough or sensitive questions. He'll bring them up before he is even asked because, just like a great salesman, he does not want to be on the defensive. Being on the defensive makes it seem like you are hiding something. You can lose rapport and the sale. Try not to be in a position where your client believes they have uncovered something you should have mentioned. Be on the offensive, not the defensive.

Bring tough topics to the forefront. For example, your competition may tell your client that the reason you are less expensive is that you use imported cheap parts. Bring it up! It allows you to answer it on your terms without being on the defensive. You can say, "We use a variety of domestic and imported parts that have passed all of our extensive testing procedures. Our goal is to provide a product that is not only the best but also offers the greatest value. Having the ability to source some parts from foreign sources allows us to reduce our pricing without sacrificing quality." Amen. When the competition tries to harpoon your deal, you'll have already created armor plating that stops anything from piercing. Get the idea?

Build a deal that can defeat all aggressors. Formulate a packaged sale so bulletproof that your client defends you. Your client can let your competition know that they are aware you are using imported parts, and they still believe your product is the best. Your competition will cringe when the buyer tells them they are aware of the situation because you have already mentioned it.

Playing devil's advocate means that you care about the buyer's concerns and want to divulge all of the bad before they ask about it. Don't go overboard with this. Great salespeople know you can take this too far. However, your experience in selling against your competition will arm you as to how much negative you can feed your client. If the competition told one of your clients that they heard that your paint peels after eight months, you can rest assured that they will say it again. It's your job to let your client know that you're aware of a rumor that your paint peels after eight months. Debunk the rumor. When your competition tries to use it against you, your buyer will already have made up his mind that it must not be true because you addressed it upfront.

Buyers want to know that you see what they see. They are already thinking about the worst-case scenario. If you can bring it up and squash his concerns, you are on your way to a sure-fire sale. The amount of "junk" you bring up prior to the close is an art form. Knowing your product, the competition, and how far you can push comes from experience.

Chapter 9

Adapt

YOU NEED TO BE ABLE to roll with the punches and adapt. As you uncover hidden truths and circumstances, you need to adapt and modify your responses. You may not be able to stay rigid on your seven-step procedure. I'm not suggesting throwing away all processes and shooting from the hip, but from time to time, situations will require you to modify your processes to keep the deal alive.

Imagine if the client's circumstances change, and he needs to postpone a purchase. You can certainly ask tons of questions to be sure there is nothing you can do to save the deal in the short term. However, you need to bend, be professional, and keep the deal alive for another day. That does not mean you should allow the client to squirm out of a deal because he is not ready. If the math works and your product is a good fit, stay the course, be firm, and close him. Remind him of all the reasons the deal is good for him. Explain that the future will likely not change his circumstances. If the product is good for him now, it should be good for him in the foreseeable future. Be staunch, but don't be a jerk. If you've determined that if you were the buyer, you too would wait, it may be time to let the deal go. Fight the fight another day. Don't hurt the relationship.

If you push too hard, you could lose the deal. However, if you play the odds and the last three out of five that you pushed ended in successful sales, I would push. Remember, sales are also a crapshoot. Nothing ventured, nothing gained. Like poker, there is a science to your odds of winning. If you play it too safe, you may never win or may win less.

We've all heard people say that they are just looking. They may say, "We are doing research and are not ready to buy." They may even say that they are simply not interested at all. How does the experienced salesperson adapt to any of the preceding? Some salespeople may ask, "Why not?" In this case, my guess is that the buyer may have an excuse like, "I need to talk to my wife first," " I don't rush into a decision," or "I need to go to three more stores first." All of these buyer objections are just excuses or canned responses that keep most salespeople from closing.

I may say something like this in response: "The fact that you're just looking, the fact that you're just doing research, the fact that you're not interested in buying now—or ever—wouldn't prevent you from looking or buying today, would it?" I may say, as I ADAPT to the situation, "If I could show you how our product or service could make you money, fix your problem, or be the perfect solution that you've been looking for, you'd consider buying today, wouldn't you?" Then, I would go into my pitch and try to sell or close them.

Sometimes, one sentence can turn a deal around. Great salespeople need to dig deep and find the one key phrase or question that resonates with a client. Clients really don't want to shop around—they are simply unsure. Clients who are not certain require coaxing and coaching; they need a nudge. I've had clients say, "I need to talk with my partner first." I may respond, "If your partner were here, what do you think he'd say?" If the client says, "I don't know," I may say, "Well, if you did know, what do you think he'd say?" "He'd probably say yes." If I got that response, I might say, "Well, it sounds like you don't need to talk with your partner." I may add, "Do you have to always ask your partner first?" or I might say, "How many times has your partner disagreed with a decision that you've made?" In most cases, the client will say, "Not very often." You can now move into a close by saying, "Why don't we do this?"

The worst thing that can happen is you get a "no," or you both agree to try to contact the partner right then. My guess is that the partner excuse is not valid anyway. The buyer is simply trying not to commit right now. Great salespeople need to push hard, keeping in mind you may never see the buyer again. Once the buyer walks out the door, the chances of getting him back are slim to none. If you want to sell, you need to use techniques that have proven success. You won't get every deal, but you will get most deals.

Have you ever had a buyer say that they think you and your product are great, but they don't think they have the money. They may say that they need to talk to his bank first for a large purchase. They may say that their credit card is maxed out. You can say, "Give me the card and let them decide," or "Other than your bank approval, is there any other reason you wouldn't buy the product or service? Is there any other reason you would buy my product or service that will make you money, is perfect for you, and solves your problem?" If they say, "Well, no," say, "Let's do this, and we'll tear up the paperwork if you don't get bank approved." You need to lasso the client while he's hot and ready. You need to strike while the iron is hot. Great salespeople seize the moment and know that the moment will pass if the client walks away.

Adapt to your circumstances, your client, and any new information that pops up as you go through the sales process. Use all of your experiences—both good and bad—and you will be on your way to being a tremendously successful salesperson.

Chapter 10

Be Honest and Sincere

SUCCESSFUL SELLING IS ABOUT SHOWING the buyer that your product or service is the perfect fit for them. It's about opening the client's eyes to all the benefits of your product or service. It's about enlightening the client that they should have purchased your product or service last year.

Trying to persuade a buyer by using sinister sales tactics, however, is a recipe for disaster. Do not swindle or lie to people. A lie does not become the truth just because people believe it. There is no reason to cheat, steal, or lie to people. Use the Golden Rule: Do unto others as you would have them do to you. I'm all about salesmanship, charm, bravado, personality, and tact when selling successfully. It's OK to use tools of the trade ethically. Some people need a "preacher's sermon" to take them to the Promised Land. Just make sure you honestly believe that where you are taking them is the "Promised Land."

Some buyers do need a kick in the fanny. They require pressure. Other buyers need some time to think about it. Be careful that you are not fooled by a buyer's excuses. Some buyers need you to help them commit. If you know the buyer should have your product, it is OK to ask, "When is the last time you spent $_____?" If he answers, "Never," you may have found the reason the buyer is hesitating. Again, you need to know your buyer by asking questions, questions, and more questions. All of the excuses a buyer will give you are just smokescreens for uncertainty. Phrases like "I need to talk to my wife," "I'm not ready," "That's a lot of money," "The dog is sick" are all smokescreens for the fact that your buyer is not certain.

It's your duty to convince them that what you have is perfect for them! You must eliminate all uncertainty by asking questions and getting his answers to help you sell to him. One way to do this is by using looping.

Looping is an art form. It refers to a sales tactic that allows you to keep "looping back" to address each and every concern a client may have. For example, your client says that he needs to think about it. You may say, "I hear what you're saying, but does the idea makes sense to you? Do you like the idea?' The client will respond with "Yes" or "No" and probably add a reason. You can then loop back and start selling the product again. You can do this over and over by continuing to ask questions and loop back. Obviously, you may have to loop back for days or possibly weeks with a more expensive or complex product. Regardless, once you know your industry, product, client base, and procedures, you'll know exactly how—and how often—to keep looping.

The bottom line: Selling is about asking questions and providing a solution to your buyer. It's about helping the buyer to "see the proverbial light. You are not doing anything sleazy or underhanded by presenting a viable, worthwhile option the client can benefit from. Keep pushing hard and asking questions.

Chapter 11

Choosing the Right Product or Service to Sell

WHAT YOU ARE SELLING IS SO, SO, SO, important! If your product is awesome and tremendously valuable, it should sell itself, right? Wouldn't that be great? Your product is vital to your success. You can learn how to overcome obstacles and be the best salesperson in the world, but be honest with yourself. If your product is horrible, overpriced, and, most importantly, does not appeal to your market, you've got an uphill battle. Who wants to have to persuade anyone to buy something that is inferior?

Try to find a product that is easy to sell. Make your life easier by either creating the perfect product or representing easy-to-sell products. Sell products that everybody wants, needs, or should have. Yes, a great salesperson should be able to sell nearly anything to anyone. But trying to persuade a buyer that you have their solution is not easy.

Remember the previous chapter? Be honest and sincere. Salespeople have gotten a bad reputation for selling bad products by using sales techniques that "bamboozle" or trick someone into buying. Focus on helping the buyer by providing him with a valuable service or product.

Now that you have a great product, how do you sell it? If you have control over the design of the product or service, you need to distinguish yourself and your product from everyone and everything else in the industry. Be different, but more importantly, be better than the rest. Make your sales life easier by creating a product or service second to none.

How can you stand out from the rest? If your product is novel, spend the time and money to get a patent or trademark. These are valuable business tools that protect you and offer exclusivity. Exclusivity can reap massive financial rewards. Being unique is a no-brainer and can effectively eliminate your competition, which is only good for the buyer, by the way. If your product is the best, unique, and helpful to your clients, you're on your way to sales success.

Make sure your product is well known. If you're going to advertise, advertise big! Go big or go home. Clients want to buy from a winner. They want to believe your product is the only solution for them. Play up the popularity, novelty, or uniqueness of your product. Popularity appeals to basic human psychology and works in sales, too. If everyone is buying it, most buyers feel it must be right. Frequently refer to testimonials when corresponding with your client. People feel more comfortable knowing that another person is happy with your product.

So how do you become the product or service your buyer really wants? Be the best at one thing (at least): value, design, uniqueness, and so on. How many times have you heard a client say that he has not heard of you or your product? If the answer is "quite often," you are not doing an effective job of marketing your product. Use all the free media tools, like social media and blog posts, available to you. Post video clips and blogs frequently. You want buyers to know you and your product before they ever meet you. You want to eliminate obscurity. It's so much harder to sell your product or service if your buyer does not know your company and what you sell.

Plant a seed in your buyer's brain. You want to engrain your product into their head. You want them to be thinking about your product when the competition is presenting their product. Give them a key phrase or something to remember you or your product. For example, "There is nothing like our product, period."

Loss aversion, the fear of losing, is twice as powerful psychologically as the desire to gain[1]. You may ask, "How much money are you going to lose by not having our product or service this month, week, or year?" The thought of losing money is extremely powerful! People are much more likely to buy when faced with loss rather than gain. People hate to lose—it is a painful emotion. Pain triggers emotions like fear, anxiety, and tension. People will go to great lengths to avoid loss. You need to sincerely convince your buyer that they will "lose" if they do not have your product or service.

If you are selling a one of a kind product you could use the scarcity principle to explain that once your product sells it may never be offered again. Scarcity and fear of loss go hand in hand in this case. How many times have you regretted not buying something like a house in a unique location that has never gone back on the market? If your product is rare and/or unique, you can suggest that not buying it may prove to be a big mistake.

The more you know about your client, the easier it will be for you to discuss the effects of not having your product on them. How do you know if your product or service will help

---

[1] https://www.investopedia.com/terms/l/loss-psychology.asp

your buyer? You need to ask questions! You need to thoroughly understand your client. (See how it all ties together?)

In general, price and complexity may also dictate the amount of time it takes to sell the product. The more complex or expensive your product or service is, the more you need to understand the buyer, your product, and the industry or demographics in which it is being marketed. It's common sense to think that it will take longer for a buyer to decide on a more expensive, complex product. You probably didn't get married after the first date. A bigger commitment takes time. That's not to say that some buyers aren't impulsive and may buy after your first date. However, you should be prepared to go the distance and tailor your presentations based on the product's complexity and price.

Your buyer will give you hints and clues about his readiness to buy. It's OK to ask a direct question about their readiness to purchase. You should use your best judgment and be tactful. It may be time to ask for the order either directly or indirectly. I prefer indirect closes like, "Has our finance department contacted you yet?" You can gather intelligence by asking questions that provide direct evidence of the buyer's interest level without asking for the order directly.

Compile a list of indirect questions that enable you to determine how much more time and effort may be required to close. There are many questions you can ask to determine your buyer's certainty level of certainty. Always remember you are trying to help him. Don't rush the sale, but do ask for the sale by asking questions like:

- ➤ If you had our product right now, could you make or save money with it?
- ➤ What address would our product be shipped to?
- ➤ Are you leaning towards working with our lender or yours?

Asking questions and getting answers gives you power! It's all about proper communication. A preacher wants to make sure the congregation is prepared to take on the week's challenges. As a seller, you want to be sure you've covered all of your buyer's concerns. You don't want to let your buyer go out into the world with doubts or the wrong message about your product. Be a good, effective preacher by discussing what challenges your client may face during the week.

You should be skilled enough in sales to mention the tough topics, including your competition, so the buyer is prepared and stays focused on your product. You may say, "I realize you are considering renting in the short term," or "I realize our competition is offering you a free vacation if you buy their product." All of these statements are designed for your buyer to offer up crucial information and tell you what you need to do to sell him. Trust me—your buyer will more than likely mention all of the options he has before buying from you.

If you haven't convinced him why you are the best option, he may ask and put you on the defensive. Selling on the defensive is hard. Say, "If I were you, I would want to be sure that all parts as well as service are available." You'll uncover so much data when you indirectly ask questions and emphasize that you see what they see. Your customers have hidden concerns and fears that you must overcome before they commit. Asking questions and putting yourself in their shoes will get you there fast and help build enough rapport to ward off your competition.

Chapter 12

Use Your Time Wisely

Try to pre-qualify your client, which can be done by various methods. Use the power of the internet to do some research. Your client may have a website, bio, or social media profiles that enable you to learn a great deal about them. If they have a website, for example, go to their mission statement to try to gain insight. Knowing who you are dealing with before you meet gives you an added advantage! Find out their religion, marital status, organization, etc. This is due diligence that many people perform on potential customers or clients. You are not being unethical by doing a little investigative work. Again, the more you know about your client, the faster you will get to the close.

If, after researching, you are still uncertain if your product is right for this client, try asking indirect questions that address your uncertainties. If you're unsure if the customer can afford your product or service, you can ask, "If you decide not to pay cash, do you have a bank relationship, or would you like to start talking with our finance team?" This may uncover financial concerns if they exist. Try to find this out without being obnoxious. Once you destroy your rapport or insult the client, you have an uphill battle—or it may simply be over.

Speed is vital in sales. You've heard the expression, "Strike while the iron is hot." Essentially, people have short attention spans. Buyers have little time to waste, and you have less time to convince them that they need your product. When a client is in "buy" mode, you need to focus and be as brief as possible. Do not waste their or your time. The iron will not be hot forever.

You've probably heard people say that buyers buy with emotion and justify with logic. Emotion is short-lived. When buying an expensive or complex product, you may have less than 30 days. In fact, you may have only three hours! Time is precious, and you need to get to the point quickly. Show the client that you are professional by staying on topic.

Ask the hard, more intrusive questions if things seem at a standstill. Remember, you want the sale! Don't be afraid to ask hard, targeted questions and push. If you're going to lose a deal, lose it on your terms. You'll sleep better at night knowing you uncovered the real reason the client is not buying. For example, you can say, "Mr. Smith, you mentioned that you need to think about the last two times we met. Are you the only one making the decision? Have you spoken with your lender or ours? What other options do you have?"

When the client answers, you may need to push even harder. Remember, your job is to uncover why the client is not buying. If they say, "I'm not sure" or "I just need more time," you need to push further and say, "I hear what you're saying, but are you unsure about our product or service? Can you not picture yourself using our product? How much money will you lose next month by not having our product?" You can push more than you think if you've established the proper rapport with your buyer. The more he trusts and respects you, the harder you can push. Some people will actually appreciate you pushing them. They psychologically don't want you to let them off the hook.

Some buyers will only move forward if you create perceived pain, a deadline, or fear of loss.

Always use time to your advantage. However, there are circumstances that can and will affect the time it takes to sell your product. There are instances when a decision cannot be made ASAP. In these cases, you will use time differently to close the deal. For example, a more complex, expensive product may require multiple conversations, more research and product demonstrations, and the transfer of various data sheets to ensure a buyer that this investment is prudent. A salesperson has to gauge the amount of pressure that should be applied to a client buying this more, expensive product. In this scenario, it can be an art form to apply pressure without being too pushy.

You want to inflate the balloon, being careful it doesn't burst. I've found the best way to do this is to continue to ask questions. Ask your buyer where they are in the decision-making process or what additional data or information you can provide to assist them in moving forward. They will give you all the information you need to apply the right amount of pressure. Sometimes, you may need to "back off" for an hour, a day, or possibly longer. Time might change how a buyer feels about your product. There is always a risk that the client will not think about your product at all if you "back off" for several days, but consider your deal intact as long as the client continues to communicate. You can ask the client to promise you not to do anything before consulting you first. Clients normally respond by saying, "Sure, I won't do anything without talking with you again." Hastily pushing your client or appearing desperate can actually have the opposite effect. They will sense your anxiousness, which can, in turn, make them nervous.

You can apply some pressure by saying, "I know this product is the perfect fit, but I realize you may need some time to think about it." Add that your lead times continue to increase, and you want to be sure he gets your product when he needs it (again, using the concept of time). This technique allows you to apply pressure while conveying that it is up to the buyer if he wants to wait. You can loop back and say, "Why not do it now? You're going to do it anyway. There's no reason to delay. You're always busy, and this makes sense." Keep the client on the hook by saying, "It's up to you," but adding comments that encourage him to move forward <u>now</u>. Tell them you're ready when they're ready.

Patience in a deal is a virtue. Clients will sense if you are antsy. Keep calm, cool, and collected at all times. Tell the client that they are the boss. It's like parenting children—sometimes, the harder you push, the longer it takes to get things done. Be patient and make sure to emphasize to the client to keep you informed of any concerns they have.

You want to be sure that you don't leave them alone for too long; otherwise, you could risk that they will start working with your competition. In addition, if you wait too long to follow up, you may have to start the entire process over again from step 1. Use different forms of communication to remind him that you exist. For example, you may text him that you heard the Yankees won last night if he's a baseball fan. Be creative and think of unique ways to let him know you're around. Email him a story or photos of the last product that you delivered. Stay in front of him, and remind him about you and your product. You should use regular mail, text, email, and phone calls to stay in touch. Too much of one method could exhaust or upset the client.

Remember, you don't have to discuss the product to stay in touch with them. He'll remember you and your product or service when you send him a muscle car video or something that he is interested in. I like to use stuff like, "Hope you had a wonderful Memorial Day!" It's an indirect way to build rapport while staying in touch. You could say that you heard the banks are raising interest rates in the next 30 days. If your product is large enough to require financing, this could spark the client to move quicker. Get creative. You're asking but not asking. Let's face it; the client probably knows why you are staying in touch.

Remember that some clients will require more time than others. You could make notes about each client and how much time you feel they will need to decide. Keeping track of where each client is in the process will enable you to categorize and structure your sales leads and prospects. The more organized you are, the better your sales will be. Also, keep track of the various communication methods you use for each client. Automate your approach as much as possible, and fill up your pipeline with the most leads.

Deals can be fragile, and your experience and wisdom will increase over time—and so will your patience. You'll learn to adapt to the needs of each client. Clients are like recipes. Some will take more time and effort. Speaking of cooking, consider how you time each dish when cooking a multi-course deal. The potatoes may take longer to cook than the toast. In the end, you want to eat it all without burning anything. Similarly, you want to land each client without burning your deal. Be patient and stick with your process to achieve maximum results.

Chapter 13

The Smokin' Sales Process

SALES CAN BE SIMILAR TO smoke. They don't necessarily linger long and can have infinite patterns. It can be hard to breathe in. It rarely follows the same path. It normally leads to fire—or you selling something. You're looking for the fire as a salesperson.

It's not always easy to stick to a rigid script when selling a complex, more expensive product, but being consistent can help streamline and automate parts of your process. Be prepared to deviate as clients' needs dictate. You may have to follow the smoke, no matter where it takes you. So, how do you know where to go?

I let the answers each client gives dictate the direction. If the client mentions he has financial issues, I follow the finance path. If the client says he is researching the competition, I drop the script and start to discuss the competition. I am spraying water on the "smoke"—the answers the client is providing. I'm trying to contain the smoke or at least follow it to where the fire (sale) is.

Much like a mixed martial artist, you know rigid techniques to defend, hit, and hold. However, once you're in the heat of the fight, you have to use your training and deviate from a rigid sequence. You may have to defend, hold, and then hit. You may have to hit, defend, and then hold. You will have to change your fighting tactics to match what your opponent is doing. Similarly, in sales, you need to modify your approach from time to time. This doesn't mean you throw away all of the training you've learned. It simply means that you must pull from (extract) your training knowledge and use it in the appropriate time and sequence. The more complex your sale, the more training you'll need to close. Experience comes from trial and error.

There are times where you will lose a deal, and that is OK. Learn from each and every loss. Wisdom comes from experience, and the more experiences you have, win or lose, the more wisdom you will have. Your wisdom will get you through any deal or negotiation.

Chapter 14

Sell Like You're a Natural-Born Salesperson

CREATE AN AURA ABOUT YOURSELF that screams professionalism, knowledge, and caring. If you're not a natural salesperson, you may have to work harder. I believe that some people are born with a natural sales ability. Think of some professional athletes who just seem to be naturally good at their sport, like they don't have to train at all (though, keep in mind that this likely isn't the case). Some people are simply born with a God-given talent for something.

Donald Trump has spent hours training on how to give speeches to the American public. He's been trained by the best and still will never be Ronald Reagan or Bill Clinton, who were natural-born politicians. They knew exactly when to wink, wince, smile, laugh, be serious, or say just the right thing at the right time. Some people have this ability; some can be taught, but it comes to the best naturally, excelling with seemingly little or no effort.

We can't turn copper into gold by polishing it with chemicals and a buffing wheel. We can, however, make copper look like gold. Similarly, anyone can learn and polish their skills and be successful at sales! It just may be more difficult. Remember, there was only one Billy Graham. Thousands of preachers but only one Graham. He had a God-given ability to bond with people and convey the Bible's message. There are still thousands of very successful, wonderful preachers loved by their congregation. Focus on being the best that you can be with massive effort and determination.

Everyone has something they shine at, something that makes them stand out. Thank goodness that we are not all the same! One cheat is to focus on what has made the most successful people successful. It is OK to emulate others and follow the most successful people's path. Choose them wisely and study their habits. There is no reason to start from the ground up and try to figure it all out on your own.

My suggestion is to pick the most successful people in your industry and copy what they've done. Also, get ideas from successful people outside of your industry; you may integrate them into your industry. Study their habits, read books, and watch videos by the people you admire. Great people normally have had great mentors, just like great athletes most likely had great coaches. The world is your oyster. The information age has given you access to the entire world at your fingertips.

Study successful people from the past and present. You can learn something from each and every book you read and video you watch. Time is short; fill your head with the world's best and brightest's thoughts. In your quest for knowledge, there is no room for racism and ignorance. People from all walks of life, race, religions, ethnicities, and genders are successful. Learn from them all. If you are truly trying to help all people in sales, you must overcome any prejudices you may have. Enough preaching. If your goal is to be successful in the world, you must realize the world is diverse. You will find inspiration among successful leaders and business people from all walks of life.

Dedication and perseverance are key ingredients to your quest to be among the best. Do not underestimate the amount of effort that is required to achieve success. There is no room for what I call a "slug"—someone who hangs around, complains, and watches the world pass him by. A slug is lazy and thinks that the world happens to him. A slug gives up at the first sign of failure. Don't be a slug; you must persevere. Don't take no for an answer.

Be committed to achieving your goals and dig deep with questions that will reveal your client's true motives and reasons for their behavior. If you require a reminder of what perseverance and dedication look like, simply watch a marine training session. Watch videos on professional athletes' training. Read books and listen to the stories of the most successful people and what it took to achieve their goals. You'll be blown away at the massive amount of effort required to be the best. Choose your heroes for inspiration and mentorship.

Chapter 15

Mindset

You've got to get yourself into the right frame of mind. Nobody can be at their peak level every minute of every day. Some circumstances are out of your control. Some people around you will not share your enthusiasm or goals and can bring you down. You are only human. Your associates, the media, and even your friends or family can influence your mindset.

Surround yourself with people who inspire you, who will boost your spirits. Your friends should be proud of your accomplishments and encourage you to be all that you can be. Good friends are happy for you and there when things are tough. Jealousy, hatred, and pettiness have no place in a healthy friendship. Choose your friends wisely. Everyone who surrounds you can have a significant impact on your mindset—positively and negatively. Integrity is at the core of it all. You need everyone and everything you surround yourself with to constantly inspire you and encourage you to persevere.

Obviously, a positive attitude is incredibly important. It's like wearing armor into battle. You never know when you'll need it, so it gives you peace of mind knowing that you possess it. You also feel prepared to take on the world. Stay upbeat! Sing a song, whistle, skip, and turn off all negativity that you can control. Remember, you are in control of most of what you take in.

To be a leader—and ultimately successful—you need to follow the beat of a different, "positive" drummer. If you need a dose of inspiration, go to church, listen to inspirational gurus, just soak in the positive. You don't have to believe every word or be inspired by every story to get something out of each and every source of inspiration. Positively will exude from you in all your interactions with others. People are drawn to that.

Similarly, your client's frame of mind is important to a successful deal. Some knowledge of your client's recent good news can be beneficial. If the client is in a good mood, it may be an opportune time to approach him. For example, your client was recently awarded a bid. Time to call him! Positive events or simply waiting for a sunny day may tip the scales in your direction. Buyers who are in a positive frame of mind are much more likely to buy.

I typically do not contact buyers on Monday morning. Most people are a little more down or stressed on Mondays. We think about all we have to do at the start of a new week. Timing your approach for a more appropriate time is prudent. Wait until after your client has had his morning coffee. In essence, try to time your approach when your client is in good spirits and less stressed. You will both be more at ease, and your meeting will be more fruitful.

Never give up. Stay the course. Go for it. Go BIG, or why go through the wonderful journey of life? Never be satisfied, strive for success, and don't let anyone stand in your way. It's tough. Don't let anyone convince you that life should be easy. Yes, from time to time, there are times of glorious reprieve, which should appreciate and bask in those moments. They may be fleeting, but they will come again.

Appreciate your good health. Be happy for others, and stay positive throughout adversity. Thank Almighty God for what you have. I can assure you there are many others who would love to be in your shoes. You can visit a hospital on any day to see where you could be. Grab onto life with both hands and see where it takes you. Make the effort, do the work, and blaze through the tough times. Be patient but persevere. Massive effort is required. Trust me; the successful people around you have been on a long, arduous journey. What you see on the surface does not tell you the whole story of a successful person.

Once you achieve success, people will say, "It must be nice," or "You're so lucky." That's fine. I would expect people to be jealous or assume you did very little to get where you are. I've heard successful people say to those who want to be in their shoes, "You want to be in my shoes with my level of success, BUT do you want to do what I have done to be in my shoes?" This is the ultimate question.

Caffeine cannot be a substitute for morning inspiration and a positive attitude. The combination of good food, caffeine, and your mental state will sustain you and get you through the day. Remember to stay focused and don't lose faith. Shoot for the stars; whatever you land on is still a high mark. It's better to set your goals too high and miss them than to set your goals too low and hit them. Underachievers will make excuses and complain about their circumstances. Achievers simply go around obstacles and do everything in their power to improve their situation.

Possess self-discipline in everything you do. Have the self-discipline to eat healthily and work hard and work out. Healthy habits not only help you live longer, but they also enable you to live a healthier, happier, more abundant life. Your health gives you strength, patience, and endurance, and to be great at sales, you need energy. You also have to exude confidence and positivity to those you are selling to. Your personality and overall demeanor are incredible assets. Be confident but not cocky. Be pleasant and approachable. Being pleasant is harder than it sounds. It does require a bit of restraint.

Chapter 16

My Cheat Sheet: Quick Reference Techniques and Fast Responses

WE'VE DISCUSSED CONCEPTS AND THEORIES. Now it's time to provide actual phrases and scripts that will enable you to become a top sales professional. Focus on the ones that best fit your specific needs.

Remember that what actually prompts a buyer to buy or triggers a response from them can and will vary for each individual buyer, so what sales tactic and script you choose may vary slightly. Keep plugging the benefits of your product while exposing his pain points. Ask him, "What will happen if you don't have my product or service? Will you continue to experience a loss? Are you willing to risk losing the profits we have discussed because you didn't have the product?" Eventually, you should invoke a response that will force them to react. Each buyer will have some hidden trigger that sparks them to act. Your job is to find it!

Know what type of buyer you have.

Buyer types:

1. "I need" buyer
2. Bargain hunter
3. Impulse buyer
4. Wandering buyer
5. Habitual/seasonal buyer

*Sometimes, they can be all five at the same time.

Move all types of buyers to be a "now" buyer! Remember that most buyers are not rational, and like the title of this book states, they "ain't right!"

There might be hidden concerns your client will have after all is said and done. If so, you will definitely have to address each of them. If your client is hung up on the price, you need to do everything you possibly can to remind them of the reasons your product will be beneficial. In some cases, you may be at a standstill. I would not suggest saying, "What can we do?" It makes it seem like you can do something with the price, right? If your client asks you to reduce the price, you could respond using a downward inflection in your tone and say very calmly, "How am I supposed to do that?" or use starting phrases such as, "It seems like," "sounds like," or "feels like."

Here are some examples of how to use these in conversation.

<u>It seems like...</u>

➤ It seems like something is holding you back.
➤ It seems like you're having concerns about the product or service.
➤ It seems like your wife is not on board. (This one is great because if it is NOT his wife, he may say, "It's

not my wife. It's my brother." You just got him to give up everything. You flushed out who is blocking your deal.)

It sounds like...

➤ It sounds like there's something on your mind.
➤ It sounds like you've really got your guard up.
➤ It sounds like you're afraid to speak.
➤ It sounds like you're riding the fence.

It feels like...

➤ It feels like you're passionate about this.
➤ It feels like you need to speak with someone else first.
➤ It feels like you know you should do this.
➤ I'm sure it feels like we're wasting your time? (This is a hidden question. If he says, "Yes, you are," you can explore this. If he says, "No," he will elaborate and give you information.)

*Additional Techniques:

Indirect and deliberately false questions are great information gatherers. For example, you may say, "It seems like Jane is having second thoughts." The client may respond, "Yes, she is," or "It's not Jane. It's my friend Steve." Or the client may say, "Actually, we just lost a job we had bid." No matter what, throwing out a <u>deliberately false question</u> can provide a ton of information. You may say, "It sounds like your bank is having a problem approving your loan." The client may say, "Yes," or they may say, "Actually, I got approved but don't like the terms." You could then say, "It feels like I, the salesman, haven't done a good job of explaining our product to you?" The client may respond, "Yes, I still don't understand how it will help me," or he will offer up the true reason like, "No, you've done a great job. It's my father who is not convinced."

Sometimes, you need to use indirect, deliberately false statements or questions to evoke a true response. It is a sleuth tactic that can be very effective and get to the root of the problem quickly! Something is always hidden on both sides in every deal. It's your job to uncover what's hidden.

Additional Techniques to Close the Sale

Try not to use why questions. Rather, try using how or what questions.

Examples:

- ➤ How do you think I could do that?
- ➤ How do you want to proceed?
- ➤ How do we fix this?
- ➤ What can we do to repair it?
- ➤ What did you have in mind at the start of our conversation?

"How" and "what" questions empower people. Make the buyer feel that they are in control by asking them how or what questions. Then follow up with something like, "You're the boss. You let me know what's best for you."

Word Substitutions to Soften the Sell

You might substitute certain words to make them softer or more acceptable to your customer. Using terminology that does not create fear, anxiety, or, worse yet, a "no" can be very helpful.

Examples:

> ➤ Use "total investment" instead of "price"
> ➤ Use "initial investment" instead of "down payment"
> ➤ Use "Agreement" instead of "contract"
> ➤ Use "approve" instead of "sign"
> ➤ Use "when you own" instead of "buy"
> ➤ Use "acquire or deliver it" instead of "sold"
> ➤ Use "areas of concern" instead of "objections"
> ➤ Use "opportunity or transaction" instead of "deal"
> ➤ Use "challenge or concern" instead of "problem"

More Tactics to Close the Sale

Be respectful during the entire sales process. Clients like to feel like partners in a deal. Never become antagonistic or argumentative with them. You should always acknowledge and agree while making persuasive suggestions. Clients are more receptive to your ideas if they feel you agree with them. Even if you disagree, they need to feel like you understand where they are coming from.

During the sales process, elaborate and use words that show you're listening. If the client is talking about the last job he completed in record time, you should reply with, "Wow!" or "How did you do that!" You can use subtle cues, like "Oh" and nodding your head to reinforce that you're listening. This is NOT a time for you to compare yourself to them or try to one-up them. I've heard many salespeople start talking about their accomplishments after the client talks about theirs. For example, if the client is talking about his son who was in the Army, you should not say, "My son is a Marine." (However, in some instances, showing how you're similar can build rapport and connection—but only at the right times.) The sale is not about you. There is no time to brag about you, your family, or your life.

Look for ways to tie the benefits of your product or service into your client's accomplishments. How might it help them be even more successful? Relate your product's benefits to your client's needs. In the above example, if he says he finished his last job in record time, you can say, "Most of our best clients have found that our product or service has been a tremendous asset to getting jobs done faster." Tie your product to what is important to your client. Be truthful, and remind him that what you are selling will help him.

Simple interjections from time to time will pique and keep his interest. Listen more than you speak. You have two ears and one mouth for a reason. When you are speaking, make sure to pause and let him respond. Don't be afraid to use the old "effective pause." They call it effective because it is. It also shows that you care about what he has to say. Remember, you are still asking questions, learning, and gathering vital information to close your sale.

Use the following steps:

Step 1: Ask questions.
Step 2: Present your offer.
Step 3: Ask questions to close the sale.
Step 4: Ask for the order.
Step 5: If the client objects, then loop back to step 2 or 3.
Step 6: Ask for the order again.

More Sales Tips:

- **Role play** after sales calls with colleagues. Learn how to improve. Tape or record your conversations and play them back to glean more insights.
- The phone is still the best sales tool. Call, call, call.
- Be honest.
- Be interesting and interested.
- Believe you can sell on the first call. However, 5–8 calls is more realistic.
- Remember that the client is always right. At least, they think they are.
- Validate their concerns. You can say, "That's a very valid concern. Many of our best clients had that exact concern before they bought." Then, tie it into how your product helped address it.
- Be complimentary.
- Use the client's NAME often when talking. Their name makes them feel important.
- If a client calls in, you should immediately start asking questions.
- Create a script for all calls, like the example below:

>   Good morning! This is Bob. Can I help you?
>   Let me know a little bit about what you are trying to do?
>   How long have you been thinking about crushing or recycling concrete or asphalt?
>   How much material do you have?
>   What size(s) would you like to produce?

*Note: Once your initial questions are answered, you can briefly outline what you offer. For example:

> The Rebel Crusher has been specifically designed for the U.S. military to build roads. We have Rebel Crushers in Afghanistan, Iraq, Iran, and all over the Middle East. They're also in Africa, Australia, South America, and numerous other military bases all over the world. The Rebel is designed so that an 18-year-old soldier with no experience in crushing or recycling can run it. It's incredible how simple it is to operate!
>
> It's a one-man operation. You can put the remote control in the cab of the loader and run the entire machine from inside the loader. You can track it around a building or up on a ramp. You can adjust the speed of the feeder all from the remote control. The Rebel can handle huge chunks of concrete loaded with rebar. It'll produce beautiful base material or up to four different products at the same time! You can make 1, 2, up to 4 different sizes, plus the magnet will make a separate pile of scrap steel.
>
> It's amazing! We've got Rebels all over the world. We've got them in NYC, Chicago, California, everywhere. It's incredible! It weighs less than 20 tons, so you can move it anywhere with no permit.

We are privileged to have an incredibly descriptive language that does not limit us to using only simple adjectives and adverbs to describe things. Be flowery, and use the full potential of our amazing, robust, extraordinary, spectacular language. Use simple words, such as "good" and "bad," sparingly. Try using "wonderful" and "horrible," for example. Study a thesaurus, and use words like weapons to battle clients. The more powerful your words are, the more chances you have of closing the sale. People remember poignant sayings and phrases because they capture their attention. The more unique and descriptive the words, the more effective your message will be. Only one sentence or phrase may entice a buyer to move forward.

Examples of impactful descriptive words and phrases that work:

- Awesome, unusual, amazing, tremendous, phenomenal, killer, incredible, ridiculous, best thing since sliced bread
- Save, avoid, fix
- Simple
- Because
- First, now
- Imagine
- Unbelievable value, free
- We, our, together, us
- We can

Two examples of final sentences to use before attempting to close:

1. A big part of the Rebel's success is that it's an incredible value!
2. Most people get into the machine for around $3700–3900/month. You'll make that in one day! There's nothing like it. We've made millionaires out of people.
3. Based on everything we've discussed, the Rebel Crusher is a perfect fit for you, John.

Once your questions have been answered by your client and you've presented your offer, including your final sentences, it's time to start to close. Closing is the act of asking for the order tactfully. Obviously, if there is no objection by your client, you should move to documents and payment discussions.

How to Respond If You Get A Common Objection:

You may hear objections such as: Let me think about it; I need to talk to my wife, I need to see how much material I have." Yada yada yada.

OBJECTION: It's more than I want to spend.

RESPONSE: It may be a little more, but it's an incredible value. Some of our BEST clients thought it might be a little too much for them. Once they started making money, they knew they made the right decision.

➤ Most people compare the Rebel to the large $500K machines. We are closer in production and HP to the larger, more expensive machines. However, the Rebel has the feed opening and the horsepower of a larger machine while being a compact system. The Rebel is right in the middle of the tiny, imported machines and the monstrous, expensive machines. The Rebel is the perfect size.

Other responses to objections may look like the following:

If we do step-by-step, apples-to-apples comparison, the Rebel has NO equal...

➤ I hear you. The best normally has a higher price. However, your cost per year to own the best will be less.
➤ Do you believe we have answered all of your questions? Is the Rebel right for you? Do you believe the Rebel will meet all of your needs?
➤ How much will it cost you to do nothing?

- Is it a cash flow issue or a budget issue? If budget, let's get creative with a finance package that is more acceptable.
- Mr. Smith, when you say it's a budget issue, does that mean you don't have the money, or you have the money but don't want to use it?
- Why don't you take it? You know it makes sense. Let's do this.
- Is your waste problem and expenses associated with waste removal going to go away by not doing something?

Keep in mind that sometimes silence is your best response.

You may say, "I hear what you're saying" or "Does the idea make sense to you? Can you imagine how much money you could save or make by not hauling the material away? It's got to be costing a fortune to haul it, pay dump fees, and possibly buy and haul rock back from the local quarry."

Looping Back...

- When you first saw the Rebel Crusher, how did you think it could help your business?
- How much will it cost you NOT to have the Rebel?
- Based on your needs, it's a perfect fit for you.
- I hear what you're saying. Does the idea make sense to you?
- Other than "X," what would prevent you from moving forward?

What to Say If Cold Calling:

"Hi, is __, there?" (Always use the first name only. If you use the customer's first and last name, the person answering the phone will automatically assume you do not know the person you are asking to speak with.)

You may reverse the order from time to time. I've had mixed results introducing myself first. I may say, "Hi, this is Bob with Rebel Crusher. Is Joe there?" I would not pause and wait for the person to ask who is calling. People feel more relaxed when you offer who you are upfront. If they do not want to patch you through to Joe, then ask them what they suggest you do to reach him. Your best shot at getting through is to ask for the client and introduce yourself, all in one swift sentence. Slow down and speak clearly and confidently, like the client knows who you are. This is the most effective way of getting through. Be patient and diligent. You need to be persistent and have thick skin. Good luck!

Once the actual client is on the phone, go right into the following. Don't ask how they are or talk about the weather.

This is Bob with Rebel Crusher. _____, the reason for the call today is_____.

If the client says, "I'm not interested," you might say, "I know that! Why would you be? <u>I take full responsibility for that.</u> Aside from that, is there any other reason you wouldn't give me five minutes?"

OR

> *"I hear what you're saying, _____. Does the idea make sense to you?"*

If the customer asks your price in the middle of your script, you might say, "It's a cash outlay of only $_____. Let me tell you exactly what you're going to get for that: You're going to get (benefit one), (benefit two), and (benefit three). Again, getting started is simple, so believe me, if you do even HALF as well as the rest of our clients, then the only problem you'll have is that we didn't get started six months ago."

> *"Now, _____, getting started here is very simple. We will do everything in our power to ensure that the process goes smoothly. It's just a question of your name and some other basic information, and then we handle everything else for you on this end. When you combine our incredibly simple and smooth process with (benefit one), (benefit two), and (benefit three), then, believe me, _____, the only problem you're going to have is that you didn't buy two of them."*

*What to Say at the Beginning of a Second Call or Contact Point:

- ➤ John, The reason for the call today is _____.
- ➤ I know you weren't expecting my call.
- ➤ Is this a bad time to talk?
- ➤ Thank you for taking my call.

Use the 4 Ps When Selling:

1. **Promise** – Address in the first sentence (fast and quick), such as, "Nobody will offer you greater value!"
2. **Picture** – "Picture yourself using the machine." Focus on the client's emotions. Remember, clients buy with emotion and justify with logic!
3. **Proof** – Show them; don't tell them. Offer visual examples and written testimonials from clients. Validate your claims. Combine client testimonials and referrals with online videos depicting their positive experiences.
4. **Pitch** – Give them one thing that makes your product or service superior to all others.

How to Handle On-the-Fence Clients

- You can say, "I can see that you are on the fence. What do I have to do to get you on our side?" Apply pressure.
- After 2–3 contacts with a client, you can say, "You are not making a rash decision. We've discussed all of your options on several occasions. We know this is the right machine to solve your problems. You have done all of the research. It's time to move forward."
- Raise a client's certainty and confidence. Many clients will not buy because they are uncertain.
- Ask the client, "Have you ever made a bad decision?" If the client answers, "Yes," ask the client to explain it. Then say, "You survived the decision. You're still in business. This is a completely different scenario. Don't let a previous bad decision prevent you from making a future great decision. Let's do this!"

➤ If the client answers, "No," or "Maybe a few," you can say, "John, you are qualified and have proven you are a good decision-maker. This is another good decision with numerous benefits for you."

Helpful Tips and Phrases:

➤ Sometimes, it's best to give a price range rather than the exact price. Then ask, "How do you feel about the price?"
➤ "What other machine(s) are you looking at?" If they don't volunteer the information, you can mention that "We've seen some Chinese and European machines priced at $150K. Let's compare apples to apples."
➤ "I will only sell you what you want. I won't oversell you."
➤ "Let me show you what other people are buying."
➤ Find out what the competition won't do and DO IT!

Handy Phrases to use when Qualifying a Buyer:

➤ " How do you feel about the price? What do you think the Rebel Crusher price is?"
➤ "What were you thinking of spending?"
➤ "Are you the decision-maker? Do you need to consult with anyone else?"
➤ "Do you need to talk with your wife or partner? If so, what do you think he or she would say right now?"
➤ "If I show you the return on investment, are you OK with a 20% down payment?"

3 Things Buyers Must Have to Move Forward:

1. 1. They must be the decision-maker.
2. 2. They must have some sense of urgency (e.g., they are losing money each day by not having the machine).
3. 3. They must be qualified. In other words, they must be able to afford your product or service.

More Possible Client Objections and How to Deal with Them:

Let me THINK about it…

➤ When a client says that they want to think about it, there are usually one or two reasons.

1. He's not interested
2. He's interested but not sure.

➤ Three questions to ask if they are not sure:

1. Does it fit their needs?
2. Is it functional for them with the features they need?
3. How do they finance it?

Depending on how the client responds in the above exchange, it may be time to ask for their business and try to close them.

It's "too expensive" is one of the most common comments you'll hear. There are numerous ways to handle this phrase—90% of the time, it is NOT an objection but rather a complaint. Use your instincts to determine the proper response. Do not be argumentative! Focus on what the client may be <u>losing</u> if the Rebel is not onsite. The fear of loss is stronger than the desire for gain. Try to create brain pain: "If you don't buy this product, you are losing $X per hour. By renting or running the wrong machine, you are losing $X."

Responses and Closing Sentences:

1. "I hear what you're saying_____, but does the idea make sense to you?"
2. "Many of our clients felt that way in the beginning."
3. "I agree. I take full responsibility for that. Let me ask you a question. When is the last time you spent $200K?"
4. "Help me to understand what you mean, Mr. Smith."
5. Cost vs. price response: "Are you concerned about the cost or the price?"

    Explain that you knew a client who bought the wrong machine because the price was lower. It broke down every day. It cost him far more in downtime and repairs than the price difference of the better, slightly more expensive machine. "I'm sure you didn't build your business by only buying the lowest-priced items. You are too wise not to consider the cost of owning the wrong machine. Remember, if you buy the wrong machine at a discount, it still means you bought the wrong machine! Our price may be little higher, but nobody beats us on cost."

    "Price is a one-time thing. However, buying a cheap product will likely cause you to pay frequent and costly repair bills. Overall, cheap products tend to have a higher lifetime <u>cost</u> of ownership. The real question is, 'Don't you want the best possible cost?"

6. "Help me understand what you mean? Why do you feel that way?"
7. "Thanks for sharing that with me. Other than price, do you have other concerns?"
8. "Thanks for the honesty. How much were you thinking of spending?"
9. "Will price keep you from getting what you want?"
10. "The best products are often more expensive. Many of our clients felt the same way in the beginning, but they all ending up buying."
11. "Let me ask you something. If money were no object, would the Rebel Crusher be the perfect solution for you?"
12. "If the money were the same between our product and the cheaper product, which one would you rather have?"
13. "You're not spending money. You're making an investment in your business!"
14. "I totally agree with you, John." I take full responsibility for that. Other than the price, is there any other reason you wouldn't buy the Rebel Crusher?"
15. <u>Use the great phrase "other than"</u>
    Examples:
    "Other than _____, is there be any other reason we would not move forward?"
    "Other than _____, that wouldn't keep you from looking, would it?"
16. "I'd hate to see you wait another year. Let's do this!"
17. "We're ready. Are you?"

18. "If I could get you 1% interest or a seven-year term, could you buy it today?"
19. "I don't have any more money to give you. However, because you are _____, I can do this…"
20. "How urgent is it to get the Rebel Crusher? Could you use it now? How much are you losing each day by not having it?"
21. "If we move forward today, I can give you _____."
22. "It seems like the Rebel is the perfect fit for you. We can get started now and put this behind you, so you can focus on your business."
23. "I've got a demo unit that just became available. It is not going to last. We have five clients who want it. Are you ready?"
24. "When is the last time you spent $X? How did it turn out? You're still in business, so it either worked, or you were able to handle the loss. Either way, this is a different deal, and it makes sense for you."
25. "Are you the decision-maker? Do you need to discuss this with anyone else? Your business partner? Wife? I talk to my wife and partners about everything. If they were here, what would they say? They'd probably agree with you, right? Let's do this now. If they don't agree, then we'll tear up the agreement."
26. "Are you pre-qualified with a bank, or do you have an existing line of credit?"
27. "Sound fair enough?"
28. "Are you ready to get started?"
29. "Are you ready to proceed?"
30. "Should we get started today?"
31. "Do we have your approval to move forward?"
32. "Do we have your approval to proceed?"

33. "Can we get your approval to proceed and move forward?"
34. "Unless you have other questions, I think we may be ready to get started."
35. "Do you have any more questions, or are we ready to proceed?"
36. "On a scale of 1–10, with 10 being ready to move forward, how ready are you to get started and buy? What reasons are keeping you from being at a 10?" Pressure the client to be closer to a 10.
37. "My question is, do you want the basic version, the pick-up tow, or the machine loaded with all of the options you need?"
38. "Mr. Smith, we seem to be in agreement that the Rebel is right for you. Are you using your bank, paying cash, or using our lender?"
39. "What can we do to speed up the process and make it happen?"
40. "How do you want the machine to be set up when it is delivered? What product(s) do you want to be making for the initial installation?"
41. "We can have it delivered by Friday. What do we need to do to make it happen?"
42. "What is the delivery address? Is the delivery address different from your office address?"
43. "What name do you want the paperwork in?"

Consider the following responses after you respond or after you have attempted to close:

➤ Use silence after a closing question.
➤ Try to answer a question with a question. The client may ask, "When can I take delivery?" You might respond, "When do you need it?"

➤ If you can't close your client, you may want to ask him, "Can you promise me that you will contact me before buying any other product?"

Emails and texts to clients must be creative. You must stand out. Always write your email focusing on how your product or service will benefit your client.

Sample emails and texts:

➤ Send singing or fun Telegrams.
➤ "Great talking with you! You are the perfect fit for the Rebel
➤ Crusher. Hundreds of Satisfied clients have made the Rebel Crusher the most popular crusher-screener in the world!"
➤ "By now, you've seen all the videos, and we've discussed the many benefits your company will enjoy by owning the Rebel Crusher. The question is, do you want the basic version or the fully loaded one?"

Atomic Emails – Use Caution Before Sending!

The following emails or texts are "ATOMIC." Atomic communication should invoke an immediate response from the buyer. However, they may also offend some buyers. If you have <u>not</u> received a response from a client after numerous attempts, the following is probably your last resort. At this point, you have nothing to lose. If the following emails do not get your client to respond, they are gone anyway.

Keep in mind that your goal is to get them to respond to you at this point. They may get ticked off, so you'll have to get creative when responding. I might say, "Mr. Smith, when we spoke, it seemed like our product was perfect for you. I didn't want you to lose out by not having it. When I didn't hear back from you, I thought something might have happened."

- "Have you <u>given up</u> trying to buy a crusher?"
- "Have you <u>given up</u> on recycling this year?"
- *Do not add any additional words or change the above emails. The term "given up," will likely force 90% of buyers to respond to you. Nobody likes to be called a quitter.

Other Tips for Being Successful at Sales and Business

- Get attention!
- Change up what you ask for. Go big, ask for more, and reduce what you are asking for only if absolutely necessary.
- It's OK to be provocative. Invoking a response or starting a debate will most likely get you noticed.
- Be passionate and committed.
- Be enthusiastic.
- Be organized.
- Prioritize and plan everything.
- Be crazy focused.
- Be persistent. Most closes take 5–8 follow-ups.
- Mix up strategies. Get creative.

    1. Phone calls
    2. Emails
    3. Referrals
    4. Demos
    5. Personal visits
    6. Social media
    7. Write a handwritten letter and mail it.

➤ Become a leader in your field.
➤ Become the go-to person.

Referrals Are Awesome!

You can ask any client or prospective client if they know anyone who can use your product. You may have to be persistent to obtain a name. Some clients may say, "I need to see if it works first." You could respond with, "No problem at all. Assuming that it does work and meets your expectations, would you be willing to provide a name or two? Out of curiosity, who is the first person who came to mind when I asked?" You can say, "I don't need a list. I only need the best one," or "If you have several, would you mind letting me know who they are?" The client will likely eventually give you at least one name.

Chapter 17

How To Purchase Anything At The Lowest Price

WE HAVEN'T SPENT TIME DISCUSSING purchasing and buying. Obviously, a business must not only be focused on selling but also on trying to save money when purchasing.

As you can imagine, most sellers are used to being "beat up" and abused. Most buyers will tell sellers that they are expensive and will criticize the value of what they are offering. As an experienced buyer, try agreeing with your seller. Most likely, they won't know what to do. You can always switch your tactic to being adversarial if this doesn't work. I like to compliment the seller on his product or service and tell them what they are offering is awesome. I may even say that it is a great value. Once I lure them into believing I'm ready to buy, I calmly mention that I'm not sure how I can afford it. I ask the seller how he can help me to buy his product or service. If there's any room for the seller to discount, they'll start reducing the price or offering various creative terms.

In any case, this tactic can be utilized to go back and forth with the seller until you know you've gotten the best deal.

After 1–2 back and forths, I may say, "It's a great product and priced right, but my budget only allows me to spend $X." I'll make it a very low, semi-realistic offer. Generally, the seller will respond with, "There's no way I can do that." This is perfect. Now, we're starting to get down to the brass tacks. I'll say, "I know, I didn't think you could." I may say, "What can you do? I do realize my budget is low." Most sellers will try to sell you a different, lower-priced product. They may even offer payment terms or discounted interest rates. Obviously, your goal is to simply get the lowest price. Continue to beat them up—nicely. After all, it's a game of seeing what the actual lowest price is. As an experienced seller, it's a joy to become the buyer. I'm finally able to turn the tables. I'll be calm, cool, and complimentary the whole time. Eventually, I'll wear down the seller without destroying the relationship.

It's all about creatively communicating. Sellers are human. They'll be more apt to help you and lower their price if you're complimentary. We've all witnessed buyers criticize the seller and the product. Bad mouthing can work, but it will be a painful exchange, trying to convince each other that one of you is wrong. There are ways to "bad mouth" a product gracefully, for example, "I love your product. Too bad it's not red. If it were red, I could buy it for your asking price because all of my other work trucks are red. Because it's not red, I have to figure in the cost of painting it." Sometimes, you need to use the word "because." The seller wants you to explain the reason you can't pay their price, especially after you've told them it's a great value.

One thing is for sure, you need to ask for a discount politely. I never tell the seller that they're crazy or wrong. I may offer valid and documented comparisons. In today's information age, I may allude to a website that clearly shows comparable products trading at lower prices. It's all about asking for a discount to be sure you're getting the best deal. If you do this each and every time you are buying something, you'll save thousands, if not millions of dollars, during your lifetime. It never hurts to ask.

Try something like this from time to time: "Mr. Seller, I love your product. You're not going to like my budget. I'm going to seem like I'm trying to steal your product." You're preparing the seller for a low-ball offer. The seller's mind will race. They may assume you want to pay half price. This is a mind trick to get the seller to start thinking of a very low offer. Once you've set the tone, you can ask for 10% or 20% off and more easily obtain it. The seller will be relieved that their assumption of a 50% price reduction is not what you're looking for.

The point is that you got their mind to start thinking of the worst possible scenario. When your offer is actually reasonable, the seller is relieved. This is very similar to breaking bad news to someone. Experts have said that mentioning upfront that you have very bad news prepares people, and they appreciate it. Think of a pilot asking you to brace for impact prior to the impact. You appreciate being warned. You're not as shocked. Whether it's buying, selling, or simply communicating bad news, your tone and how you say it matter. I don't have a problem making up an innocent story or blaming a third party, like my wife, if it will help to lower the price of what I'm buying. Deflecting the blame onto a third party is a powerful bargaining technique. It allows you to maintain rapport while casting all of the blame for haggling onto another.

After going back and forth several times, I encourage you to start using odd, more exact numbers. For example, if the asking price is $10,000, I may offer $7,727. It makes the seller feel that I have spent time calculating a precise number I am willing to pay. I may say that I've reviewed the numbers, and based on _____, this is the number that makes sense for me.

It also speeds up the negotiation process and gets the seller to focus on their bottom-line number.

Lastly, I never act like I have won in the negotiation. I may act like they have won and I have given in. It helps for future negotiating with this individual or company. It's a tactic that makes them feel like they got you to pay the most you were willing to pay.

I've only touched on some of my favorite negotiation tactics. I suggest reading books dedicated to negotiation. One of my favorites is *Getting More* by Stuart Diamond.

Chapter 18

Asking for and Negotiating to Get the Order

REMEMBER, THROUGHOUT THE SALES PROCESS, you're always gathering information and asking questions. You've built rapport and established that you're an authority in your field. You are moving further down the path to the close. As you go, you need to solidify your deal.

When selling an expensive or complex product or service, you may need to use some additional strategic tactics to close the most difficult of clients. I'm a big believer in asking for the deal, or close, numerous times along the way because it is part of your information gathering. For example, if, after the first meeting, I feel the client may be ready, I might say, "We have a two-week lead time. Can you live with that?" Notice I did not directly ask them if they're ready to buy.

I didn't say, "What do you think?" I hate that phrase; it increases the client's anxiety. You can see them start to get nervous. Do not ask an open-ended question that may make your client nervous. You can say, "It's the perfect machine for you! Do you agree?" A simple "yes" or "no" response is less stressful and simple for the client to respond to. If they say no, they will either provide more information or explain what is holding them back.

Remember, objections are a starting point, not the end. Keep prying into their mind to see what they are really feeling. If you want to sell, you must dig deeper, or your client will never give you their reason for not buying. Without the real reason, you can't explain why they should have your product or service.

The great job you did in the initial phases of meeting and greeting, establishing rapport, and questions and answers will now all pay off. If the client is convinced your product or service is perfect, further negotiation may not be necessary. If the client is still speaking with you after several meetings, they probably want your product at the price you've discussed.

However, it is possible there are hidden concerns your client still holds after all is said and done. If so, you will have to address each and every one of them. If the client is hung up on the price, you need to do everything you can to remind them why your product will benefit them. In some cases, you may be at a standstill. I would <u>not</u> suggest saying, "What can we do?" It makes it seem like you can do something with the price, right? If your client asks you to reduce the price or if you can take 5% off, you should respond with something like, "How can I do that?"

You may say, "We don't have any more money left to give you." This is slightly harsher. You may also say, "We always give our best price upfront" or "It seems like you're having concerns about the product or service." Try using various incentives rather than reducing your price. For example, you may try offering an extended warranty.

Make sure to pause and let them respond. Don't be afraid to use the old effective pause. They call it effective because it is. It also shows that you care about what they have to say. Remember, you are still asking questions, learning, and gathering vital information to close.

The buyer needs to feel like the product they are buying is worth MORE than what they're paying. The buyer has to perceive value. In other words, the buyer needs to be able to justify their decision; there could be a variety of reasons, and they may never be known by the seller. The important thing is that the transaction is taking place.

Nobody really knows what particular feature or benefit will hold the most value for a buyer. The value to the buyer could be something completely different than what the seller believes it should be or actually is. There are rare times when a product or service is purchased for reasons other than a perceived value proposition. In other words, the purchaser has another motive for buying your product or service, other than feeling it is an excellent value and necessary for their needs. Again, the buyer simply needs to have a reason to purchase that is worth more than the price of the product or service.

When a buyer really wants the product but can't or won't pay your price, a sales bridge needs to be built. I suggest using price as only one negotiating tool. Price is typically the number one consideration for buyers, but a good salesperson will uncover any and all buyer considerations. Other than price, what else may be important to the buyer? What other things may the buyer consider to be valuable? Rather than drop your price, you may offer the buyer an extended warranty, discount, or a free future service. You may offer the buyer a discount for subscribing to your YouTube channel.

You, the seller, need to be creative to get the buyer to stop focusing only on the price. Your buyer may have a time constraint. If so, then focus on a quick delivery rather than price. How much is it costing your client each day by not using your product?

Millions of products are not must-haves, that clients simply want to buy, rather than need, to buy. A sales presentation may be significantly different for these types of products. The price may have no limit. Imagine some rich guy who simply wants to buy a Picasso painting. He may pay millions more than the painting is worth. A car collector may want to repaint a perfect car because he simply wants a certain color. These decisions are emotional and more than likely are not logical.

Selling a needed product may require a more logical and mathematical sales presentation. In the end, emotion may still be the trigger that pushes the buyer to act. People buy with emotion and then justify the decision with logic. Since many buyers are not logical, the emotional stimulus may be the driving force. The first chapter, "Y'all Ain't Right," says it all.

It's OK to empower a client by asking questions that require a "no" response. Most salespeople will lead a client down a path to yes. "Do you want your business to grow? Do you want to retire someday with money? Do you want an edge over your competition?" Yes, yes, yes. Try triggering a "no" response from clients to empower them. Most people, in general, feel more powerful when they say "no." You may ask, "Is it crazy to think you could be rich?" The client will likely respond with a no. "Are you opposed to listening to the features of a machine that could make you thousands of dollars?" The client will respond with no. "Is this a bad time to talk?" The client should respond with a no. Try yes and no responses to test your client.

If there is an elephant in the room, you need to mention it. If you know the elephant exists, and it is clear they see it, don't be afraid to mention it. You want your client to explain how they feel about the elephant while they're in front of you, which allows you to explain how the elephant really doesn't matter. The last thing you want is for negative thoughts, "the elephant," to enter into your client's mind when you are not around.

Your deal should be so solid that nothing can stop it. You need to do such a phenomenal job presenting that the remaining part of your sale allows you to say almost anything. Can you imagine saying to your client, "How can you justify spending $5,000 per month on our machine?" I've done this. It solidifies a deal when you can be open and ask hard questions. The client will most likely explain in detail how they are justifying his decision. It's interesting to see what resonates in their mind as the most important reason to buy your product.

Don't assume that your buyer thinks like you do or makes decisions for the same reasons that you do. It doesn't matter what particular problem your product solves for your buyer—what matters is that your buyer feels there is something so important about your product that they must own it.

Chapter 19

Close the Door

SOME BUYERS ARE FAMILIAR WITH the tactic of anchoring, a classic tactic, during the negotiation process. To anchor simply means that the buyer makes a low ball offer to anchor or plant a seed in the seller's head that is much lower than the seller's price. The goal is to get the seller to start thinking that his price is far too high. It can work. I've always said that a buyer who uses anchoring can be referred to as a "bottom dweller." Like a catfish, a bottom dweller eats off the bottom of the lake. He only wants the lowest price and believes that price is more important than anything else.

Beware: Bottom dwellers will not consider your value proposition. They are only concerned with paying the lowest price and are not concerned about what you, the seller, think of them. Bottom dwellers must weigh the risk of offending the seller. If the seller is offended, they will mostly likely be firm, raise the price, or simply refuse to sell to the bottom dweller. Beware of low-balling a seller. It could have an adverse or opposite effect. A bottom dweller must consider if they are willing to lose it all to get the lowest price.

As a seller, you must know how to handle this type of buyer. A great salesperson knows how to handle a bottom dweller. They will not show anger or frustration or get emotional.

Rather, a great salesperson will remain calm, cool, and collected. A great response to a low-ball offer is, "How am I supposed to do that?" Similarly, a great buyer may also say, "How am I supposed to do that?" It can work both ways and is quite effective as a great way to say no while maintaining rapport. This phrase shows you're willing to listen; you're asking the other side to provide a solution. In most cases, the buyer's response will be, "Well, it can't hurt to ask," almost as if they did not expect you to consider it.

Depending on the situation, the buyer may say, "Come on, really?" Demonstrating that you are reasonable, fair, and willing to try to work with the buyer is quite effective in most instances. You can always be staunch at the end. Some people want to see how far they can push the other side to be sure they are getting the absolute best deal.

You may offer other inventory that is more or less expensive. Be careful not to entice a client capable of paying for your top product into buying a lesser product. You only want to downgrade a client who does not require or cannot afford your more expensive product. If I offer a product for less money, I clearly outline that this option does not have the top product's features or capabilities. I may say, "We have option B that is less expensive. However, it does not include x, y, or z features. We'll do whatever you'd like, but I'd hate to see you sacrifice some needed features for a few pennies." I'm being honest and appealing to the client's sense of loss.

Of course, if you haven't pre-qualified your buyer, you may find out during negotiations that they simply cannot afford your product. Shame on you, the seller. You should have determined your client's financial capabilities and needs prior to the negotiation. Does the buyer have the money? Has the buyer ever paid that much money for anything? Has the buyer ever had a bad experience when buying a similar product? Knowing that the buyer is qualified will help you be patient.

Don't be close-minded. Let the other side go first, if possible. Who knows? They may offer you more than you were expecting. A novice seller will quickly say, "Sold!" A great seller will say, "Oh my goodness!" or "Holy crap," or "You can't be serious." A great seller makes the buyer <u>feel</u> that they are getting a tremendous deal. You want the buyer to feel like they are getting your best possible price. In reality, you, the seller, know that you would have accepted less. Trust me, no buyer wants to feel like the seller was willing to lower the price.

How many times have you heard a buyer bragging about the deal they got? A buyer may say, "I stole it!" or "I worked the seller over until he finally gave in!" Conversely, how many times have you heard a buyer boasting about paying the list price? People want to feel like they got the best deal.

Make your buyer feel that they have won. There is no room—or time—for your ego in a sale. You win when you sell your product. Don't ever explain how hard you've worked for it or mention a commission. Celebrate your sale privately. When a realtor sells a $10-million-dollar home, they don't publicly brag to the home seller or buyer that their commission is worth 6% ($600,000)!

Unless it is legally required, divulging your commission can offend a buyer or seller and kill a deal—thus, the reason that many financial advisors "bury" their commission into the sale of a stock or a mortgage. People may not agree with the amount of the commission or compensation. Why risk it? Stop trying to convince your client that you are worth it. Take your commission and deposit it into the bank. Just like the Kenny Rogers' poker song says, "Don't count your money at the table."

We are all human and have a propensity to be emotional. It is only natural. Great salespeople know how to create positive emotions and responses while controlling negative emotions. Treat sales like a game. Do everything you can to increase your chances odds of closing. Don't take unnecessary risks if you want to consistently win the game.

Chapter 20

The Door Won't Close All the Way

You should NOT be negotiating during the closing. Your buyer should already be convinced that your product or service provides value. There is no reason to drop the price at this point. Remember, your buyer will question why you didn't give him the best deal if you lower the price during the closing, which, in turn, can negatively affect your rapport. If it is absolutely critical that you do something additional for your client, I suggest offering him an extra perk outside the sale of your product or service.

I was recently asked if I could do any better on a price. I've been asked why we don't offer a discount. I always say, "What kind of a company would we be if we didn't give you the best price upfront? Would you prefer that we inflate our numbers to see how much extra money we can get from you? To be fair to all of our clients, we keep our pricing consistent."

Even when you think you've sold your product, trust me, it is not a completed sale until after the money is in your bank. You can get signatures and verbal assurances, but until you get the money, your deal is still not done. How many realtors thought they sold a house after the contract is signed and earnest money is received? The fact is that the buyer can walk away anytime before the closing. Realtors will tell you not to rejoice until after the closing.

When selling anything that requires time or financing, the deal is fragile until the seller gets paid. This is a hard reality for most salespeople. They want to believe they have sold something as soon as their buyer tells them "OK." Ninety percent of the time, the sale is probably done when the buyer says, "OK," but it is the 10% that I am concerned with.

Imagine that, as a salesperson, you spent a significant amount of time and money to get the client to commit to your product or service. Once the client says, "OK," you need to recognize that you still need to be on your toes. Everything you say and do can and will affect the closing of the sale. The people in your office who interact with your client can affect a deal. Imagine if your client loves dealing with you but doesn't like your comptroller who is trying to get him to pay by wire transfer. Everyone communicating with your customer must be aware that the buyer still holds all of the cards. Everyone needs to convey the message that they value the client and will do everything they can to assist them.

Thus, this is the reason we use various techniques during the final stages of closing. We act like the deal is done whenever we refer to the product. For example, we say, "When *your* machine is delivered, our service technician will be on site." We always refer to the product as theirs. We future pace the product by acting like the machine or product is already his.

We nonchalantly discuss payment or contracts. We don't call attention to anything, even if it is critical to closing the sale. The buyer does not need to know how vital the money transfer or his signature is. Your approach should be deferential, like "no big deal." Obviously, as you near the close and the client has not done what they are supposed to do, you may have to tweak this and become harsher to get your client to comply. However, the last resort is to use a hammer to peel an onion. Treat your deal and client like you are peeling back an onion—one step at a time and with care. If you're too harsh, the client may cancel the order.

Walking clients through a lengthy closing period is an art form. Clients can and will change their mind if they don't like something while closing. Clients can get cold feet for a variety of reasons. The bottom line is to try to keep your client enthusiastic right up until closing day.

Let me give you some examples of how to navigate through some of the items essential to closing, such as payment. Your client says that they are putting a check in the mail, even though they know your terms are a wire transfer of funds. I would say something like this, "Is there any way you can send the funds by wire transfer? Our lender mentioned it might take five business days for a check to clear. We don't want to delay the closing." If you require a signature, you may say, "Did you have a chance to forward the approved documents?" Notice I did not use the words "sign" or "contract." People get nervous when anyone asks them to sign anything. The word contract also indicates the paperwork is serious and binding. Obviously, the client knows he needs to sign the contract. However, kinder and gentler terms are more psychologically acceptable for people.

If you've ever had to ask permission from your parents to go to a concert in the city, you may have used a more gentle or subtler approach. Get the idea? If you want a positive outcome, try to ensure its success by being as tactful and cautious as possible. Your words are weapons. Be careful what you say and how you say it.

You may also ask someone else in your office to contact your client. I suggest "handing off" the mundane tasks of collecting money and getting signatures. The person you handed your deal to MUST know how to handle your client. Make sure the handoff person knows what you expect them to do. One effective technique is for the handoff person to act like they are not aware if the client has followed the closing guidelines. For example, they may say something like, "Hi, Mr. Smith. I'm _____. How will you be paying today? Did you have a chance to forward your documents?"

They also need to know how to navigate possible client questions. The salesperson and the handoff person need to work together to get everything they need from the client. However, the handoff person may say, "It's my job to dot the Is and cross the Ts." Make sure this person is personable, competent, and can direct your client towards completing the last stage of the buying process so as not to derail the sale.

Chapter 21

You Thought You Had a Deal...The Client Is Still Riding The Fence

ALL SALESPEOPLE HAVE HEARD THIS, "You've done a great job. I love the product, but I still need to think about it." It's your job to dig deep and see what is holding the client back; there's normally one main reason, something that you haven't uncovered about your buyer.

If you know the product or service is perfect for him or her, push as hard as you can. Remember, a balloon can take in a tremendous amount of air before it bursts. There are dozens of client objections that are all <u>smokescreens for uncertainty</u>. For example, your client may say, "I need to talk to my partner, wife, or bank before I can commit," "I need to think about it," or "You're price is too high." Respond by saying, "I hear what you're saying, but we both know the product is perfect for you. We've done the math, applied it to your business, and it is a no brainer."

It's OK to pause at this point. It's OK to be silent for a few seconds, if not minutes. Let the client digest what you're saying. Let them speak, and be sure to listen. They may say that you're right or "I know, but I still need to think about it." I would then say, "I hear you, but what is there to think about? We've done the math. The machine is a perfect fit. You know that you need it. You know it will save and make you money. What is there to think about?"

They should offer up a legitimate reason at this point—something like, "I'm just scared to spend this much money" or "The last time I did something like this, I regretted it." This is what you want. Now, you're getting somewhere. The client is starting to share their TRUE reason(s) for not buying. You could say, "Most of our customers felt the same way. Now, they are making money, love the machine, and are so happy they didn't hesitate." You could also say, "Having not spent that much money in the past wouldn't prevent you from buying the perfect product that will not only complement your business but also provide a steady source of income and save you thousands."

You need to add pain while being truthful with your client. Keep pushing and pushing and looping and looping until the client agrees to move forward. They simply need some reassurance or a nudge. The point is to not to give up at the first sign of an objection. Remember, most clients are complaining. An objection that is not valid is a complaint and should be treated as such.

Some clients are scared, nervous, and need to be pushed. How many people need to be forced onto a roller coaster? Once the ride is over, they are ready to do it again and again. Keep using all of the closing and mind-bending techniques in Chapter 14 and 15 until the client buys. Remember, there is no money in sales. The money is in closing the deal!

Chapter 22

How to Deal With Difficult Clients After a Sale

There are so many books about the psychology of dealing with unhappy or difficult clients. I don't think it is nearly as hard or complicated as some of the "gurus" profess it to be, but it does require you to honestly care about your client. For our purposes of good and not evil, I will enlighten you as to my methods of handling even the worst clients.

It's simple. Use the Golden Rule when dealing with others: Treat others as you would like to be treated. Think of how you would want to be treated when if you were an irate customer (and rightly so in your mind). Think of what you would expect from a company you are doing business with.

Also, remember that phrase I mentioned earlier, "Y'all ain't right." As painful as it is to mention, it is possible that you can apply the Golden Rule and still not appease your client. You simply <u>cannot reason with an unreasonable person.</u>

At all times, remain calm and professional. After all, you erupting and screaming will only pour gasoline onto the fire.

If you have any chance of reasoning and satisfying your client, it is important NOT to give them any reason to perceive you as a jerk. You don't want to increase your client's frustration and anger. Don't curse or raise your voice unless it is absolutely the very last resort.

Negotiating a settlement and appeasing an irate client can be handled through the same basic strategy. Similarly to when you sold your client a product, you should ask questions that convey the message that you care. Whether it's before or after the sale, questions will allow your client to tell you what is on their mind. Let your client know that you are writing down what they are saying to be sure you address each and every concern. In addition, you should assure your client that your sole purpose is to see what you can do for them. If the client is really ticked off and is saying that you don't care about clients, you could use this phrase, "I can assure you that if I didn't care about you, I would not be having this discussion with you." If you want to add some "flowers" to the discussion, you may say that they are one of your best and most valued customers. Everyone wants to feel special and appreciated, and people want to hear that you value their business.

You need to listen to the good, the bad, and the ugly. Don't interrupt unless the client is a raving lunatic. I suggest treating your client like a fully inflated balloon ready to pop. If you add more air/anger to the discussion, they will explode! Allow your client to deflate by allowing them to talk with you and express their concerns. Once the client has finished venting, pause and be silent for a moment to show you are listening and have taken it all in and that you are digesting what they are saying. Now, you provide a well-thought-out path to a solution.

This may require that you use the same "strategic empathy" that you used during the sale. You may have to say something like, "It seems like you feel that we don't care about you. It probably seems like all we cared about was selling you something, and you feel like we don't provide the proper service and support." Just like in the sale, you are looking for the client to say, "That's right." If he says, "That's right," you are in the home stretch.

You are deflating the balloon by putting yourself in their shoes and reiterating what they are saying. Keep in mind that this is a strategy that, if done properly, will get you off the phone and/or to a conclusion much <u>faster</u> than arguing with your client. Eventually, you'll have to decide what you are willing to do to satisfy the client. Before you take a firm position, I suggest providing 1–3 partial or total solutions that they may choose from. This empowers the client by allowing him to choose.

You should phrase your response like this, "Sir, we greatly appreciate your business and will do everything we can to work with you. What do you think about _____? Does this seem like a fair resolution?" I love the phrase, "Are you aware…?" For example, "Mr. Smith, I'm not sure if you're aware…?" This phrase provides your client with a potential escape route. This particular phrase reduces tension and defensiveness and triggers honesty.

Y really can't lose by using this phrase. If the client says, "Yes, I'm aware," at least you know that they know. If they say, "No, I wasn't aware of that," it opens up the entire communication process. Either way, it's a powerful way of asking a question while making a claim or statement. If you say, "We wanted to be sure you were aware," the client feels like you care about them. It can also be a polite way of making an accusation or statement. We all know we're probably not going to make every client happy or satisfied, but your goal is to make most of them happy and satisfied. Do and say everything in your power that will enable you to find a resolution.

You also need to consider your end goal in this situation. Even if the client is completely wrong, they may be in a strategic place where you simply can't afford to have them spreading negative rumors about your business. In other words, you are doing "reputation recognizance." You may want to preserve your reputation because there are numerous prospective clients where the disgruntled client is located. In this case, consider the small cost of making this client happy vs. the negative cost of the client bad-mouthing you.

Think about what you spend on advertising and your overhead. You may spend thousands of dollars trying to convince people that your product and company are second to none. If this disgruntled client is not satisfied, his reputation bashing could negate all of your hard work and expensive marketing. Think about your end goal in the entire conflict. What do you want to achieve? Strategize and always keep your eye on your company's future. Your goal is to win the game. If you offer anything to your client, outline what you expect if you implement this policy or solution.

What do I mean by that? You should outline to your client that you want something in return. You may say, "OK, if we do _____, you agree that you have been treated fairly? Mr. Smith, would it be fair to say that we are 'all good'?" You may even go as far as to say that if anyone asks what we are like to deal with, you would say that you've had some issues, but we worked it out fairly and to your satisfaction. This is vital, especially if your goal was to give the client something that you felt they didn't deserve. You may have offered this solution strictly to preserve your reputation.

Throughout the entire discussion, always remain professional and calm. Show your client respect. Focus on the goal. Also, don't be afraid to go overboard with compliments and praise for your client. Make the client feel important and unique even if they are wrong and you are ticked off. Trust me, all clients love to be told that you care about them. Explain that you want to do everything in your power to demonstrate how much you appreciate their loyalty and business. In other words, pump them up! It may seem like blarney or bull to you, but I can assure you that it works. You WIN when your resolution maintains the client relationship without giving up all of your profits.

Depending on the situation, your client may be threatening legal action. Again, there are numerous circumstances that should be considered before implementing a client resolution legal strategy. The cost of going "legal" can be bad for both sides. I try to avoid this whenever possible. The old adage that "The only ones who win legal battles are the lawyers" is usually true. It is far less expensive and time-consuming to settle with your client. I'm not saying that you should always throw in the towel, but stay focused on your goals of selling products, making money, and keeping your client relationships. Remember, you can be totally right and still lose a lawsuit.

Having said all this, if you have to go the legal route, don't do it half-baked. In other words, after you have exhausted each and every solution, tactic and ounce of rational discussion, if you go the legal route, GO BIG! At this point, you will lay waste to all of your previous attempts to make your client happy. In other words, the gloves are off! I would suggest one last attempt by telling the client that you have a top law firm on retainer, and once they choose to go the legal route, there will be no further discussions.

Isn't it crazy to think that we have to go through all of this? It just goes to show you that when it comes to money, people will do whatever they have to. Money influences and changes people's sense of right and wrong. I have experienced it all. It's part of being in business. My gift of gab and persuasive ability has limited my exposure to lawsuits and confrontations. Just remember, this is not personal; it is business. You win when you sell and maintain customers. Stay cool, be focused, and expand your business.

Chapter 23

Practice Problem Solving

ONE OF THE BEST WAYS to sharpen your sales and negotiating skills is to practice using low-impact, minor scenarios. Practice assisting your family in minor crisis remediation. First, ask if they would like your assistance. I realize this is not business or sales, but it does give you the opportunity to use your psychological knowledge and communication techniques to solve a problem. This will not only help your family member but will also help you to become a greater communicator and problem solver. After all, aren't most salespeople problem solvers?

I may assist my family member by asking several questions, like "What do you want to achieve?" or "What do you want the outcome to be?" This is a key to most negotiations. You are getting them to focus on the goal. While the goal in sales is to help and sell the client, the goal in this personal dilemma is yet to be determined. Some issues cannot be resolved, so the focus might be on figuring out how one can tolerate the situation. You can't control people who aren't "right." However, you are in control of how you cope with it.

If it's a matter of principle, I would get creative in attempting to reach the other party. I would try to create an email or message that would invoke a fear of loss in them. I may say, "John, I'm not sure if you received my messages? I didn't want to bother you, but I'm concerned. Can you contact me ASAP?" Notice, this is very clever. The goal is to be professionally provocative in order to get them to respond. By structuring your words and still asking a question, you are using Jedi terminology to provoke them into acting.

This is very similar to creative sales techniques. The goal is to reach the buyer, and your words are your tools and weapons to either start a war or peace talks. You can always escalate a discussion, so you should choose your weapons wisely and in order of the circumstances you are faced with. Not to be taken literally, I may start with a stick, then a knife, then a gun, and then lastly, an atom bomb. Keep in mind that once you drop the atom bomb, there is no turning back. You will lay waste to your deal, negotiations, and all forms of civil communication.

In addition, if you are attempting to sell the person or convince them of something, you want the person to "want" to help you. If you force help, you may get it, but they may resent you for it. Similarly, if you threaten someone, the help you get may cause resentment. In addition, the person helping you will only be motivated to do the bare minimum. Even worse, they may try to harm you at the same time.

Think of this as a challenge. In your mind, transform any dilemma into a problem-solving game. If the game has little or no negative side effects, that's even better. Problem solving and helping family members on small issues can be fun. It will also enable you to be using your sales and negotiation and persuasion skills when the consequences are lower, allowing you to relax, focus, and think more clearly. Again, make sure you've asked if they want your advice, opinion, or assistance. Once you are summoned, go for it. Game on!

Practice your skills all the time. Roleplay with fellow co-workers, family, and friends. Tell them to make it hard for you. We all know that someday we will experience a tough buyer who is borderline crazy and obnoxious. The more skills you have and the more familiar you are with handling tough situations, the more likely you will be successful at dealing with these types of clients. One thing is for sure, if you can handle the tough ones, you will breeze through the more rational, easygoing clients.

Most athletes practice so hard that the games are easy. This can work in business as well. Make your practice sessions tough and uncomfortable when there is little or nothing at stake. Then, when you enter into the sales battle of your lifetime, you will be prepared. Your training will take over, and you will reign superior. You don't rise to the occasion. You fall to your highest level of preparation and skill level.

Chapter 24

Provocative Marketing of Your Product or Service

I CAN'T STRESS ENOUGH THE NEED to STAND OUT and be unique! Whether your product has a cool feature or you have a killer financing package, you need to offer something that nobody else does. You need to get attention. In the age of social media, getting attention is less expensive; you can potentially reach a much greater audience <u>fast</u>.

We've all heard the expression that bad news travels fast, but I advocate for creating news that is not "bad" but possibly somewhat controversial. Controversy gets people talking and can draw attention to you and your product. I would even go as far as to say that getting "haters" can actually help you. Look at celebrities who do crazy and provocative things. The next thing you know, they are in the news getting attention. Before you know it, they are signing movie deals. The public is curious about controversial people.

When Howard Stern was a disc jockey in NYC, they asked people why they watched his show if they hated the filth he promoted each day. People said they listened to hear the latest filth. They were curious about what he would say or do next. Sounds crazy, but it's true. We're in the age of reality shows, and who can top the latest shocking scenario. Reality TV stars get attention by attracting haters and creating controversy. Look back to the '80s when Madonna was considered the most controversial celebrity. Today, she seems more like a nun. I'm definitely not advocating being provocative, vulgar, or crass. Use people's curiosity to your advantage. Use your knowledge of people's curious nature to help bring attention to you and your product.

How do you do this? How do you create negative attention that can also be beneficial at the same time? We've discussed how people who criticize you can actually draw attention to your website, product, or service. You've heard the expression, "There is no such thing as bad press." In other words, all news about you is probably good news for getting more exposure and attracting attention. If nobody knows you, they can't do business with you.

When you say or do something you know is controversial, you'll need to be prepared to defend yourself against those who totally disagree with you. Regardless, at least people are talking about you. The point is to do something with ethics and class to draw attention to you and your product. You can go crazy, within reason, to promote your product or service. It's fun to be creative and see what unique methods you and your team can think of to create attention. The heart of marketing is to focus on getting your product to stand out amongst all the rest.

Think about what packs a stadium the most. A formidable rivalry means that half of the fans are probably rooting for the other side and the other half are haters of the opponent. The last presidential debate between Trump and Clinton broke audience records for a political debate. Millions of people watched, mostly because they hated the other side. A huge rivalry combined with controversy created record-breaking TV ratings. Trump and Clinton certainly got attention.

Obviously, you need to be strategic and somewhat cautious about the information you pump onto the internet. Use controversy as a tool to direct traffic to you. Don't be afraid to lose some prospective clients while trying to increase the volume of people who know about you or your product. Remember what we discussed about increasing the number of people in your sales funnel? Even if your close rate decreases but your overall volume of leads increases, you will probably benefit from an overall increase in sales.

In addition, you need to take some risks and try various tactics to increase your client base. Try some controversial yet truthful ads that provoke your competition, clients, or the public into talking about you. Poking a beehive will result in some bees leaving the hive. You may get stung, but you may also get the honey.

Controversy, both good and bad, gets you noticed. Part of your marketing plan is to get people to know and think about you. You want them talking about you. At the heart of all of the books written about marketing is the common theme to be exclusive, stand out, be unique, and, most of all, dominate your market. How do you dominate your market? Start by being the authority in your field, the big dog in the industry. Buyers take comfort in buying from companies they are familiar with.

Let's face it, a company that has been around for 20 years more likely makes buyers feel more certain that the company is established and reliable. Buyers will feel that there is less risk doing business with a 20-year-old company vs. a two-year-old startup. What do you do if you are the startup and competing with well-established companies? I suggest focusing on your strengths and the established company's weaknesses.

For example, you may be the new, modern, forward-thinking company, whereas the older company has antiquated ideas or products. You can flip it and promote your product and/or service as "cutting edge" and revolutionary. Get people to focus on your strengths. Of course, there needs to be truth in your advertising and marketing. I'm not advocating that you lie or mislead.

The beauty of modern technology is that people are not just verbally communicating. The internet and social media will blow you up much faster and to a much wider audience once everyone starts commenting and debating each other.

Chapter 25

The Business of Being in Business

Trying to tie sales into everyday business is easy. All businesses are in the sales business. Whether you're in human relations, customer service, or outside sales, mastering basic sales techniques can pay huge dividends. If you're contemplating going into business, don't discount the importance of knowing how to sell.

So, let's say you want to start a business. The first step is to do some soul searching to be sure you know what you're getting into. Do not venture forward on a hunch. Don't let your emotions run wild and make a rash, impulsive decision. Just because you're a great home cook doesn't mean you're qualified to run and operate a successful restaurant. <u>Running a business—any business—is a separate skill set, generally unrelated to your natural abilities and talents and hobbies.</u>

Conduct thorough research before committing. We're in the information age, so use all of the readily available resources to assist you. Read books, listen to podcasts, and watch YouTube videos from people in the know or who have been there and done that. Try to hone in on industry-specific data. Take advice from industry experts with hands-on experience in the business you are interested in.

Consider your ideal client type and overall location. Most businesses are affected by both the location and the particular client base. Top franchises know this to be true; they perform extensive analysis and gather data related to per capita income, road access, future growth potential, etc. Data is a valuable tool for determining risk and reward potential. You must conduct extensive research prior to deciding what, where, and when to start a business.

Look at all investments and business opportunities from every angle. Ask yourself, "What if?" What if the road closes in front of my business? What if a competitor moves next door? What if the rent or taxes go up? Be conservative and analyze all potential risks. Identify possible roadblocks before you make your final business or investment decisions. <u>In some cases (like this), it's better to make no decision than the wrong decision.</u> Be pessimistic and cautious, and don't allow your emotions and enthusiasm to overwhelm your thought process.

Sound like I'm a worrywart? Sound like I'll talk myself out of nearly anything? Sound like I'm implying that you should ignore your passion and gut feelings? Actually, I understand that most people buy with emotion and justify their decision with logic. Emotion and passion need to be present when making a decision, but they are only part of your decision-making process. Passion and emotion are wonderful driving forces to keep you motivated. However, logic and data analysis will normally uncover the true potential for most investments. The numbers normally don't lie.

If you have an opportunity to work in a particular field or business prior to investing in it, you should. You will obtain valuable and essential insight. There may not be a better way to obtain hard data than to actually experience it for yourself. Consider the potential downside and be willing to face your maximum potential loss. In other words, consider the worst possible case and be willing to accept it.

We've all heard people say that they thought something would be a great opportunity. My question would be, what made them believe it actually was worthy of investing in? Many times, you'll find that people rushed to judgment, and it cost them dearly. They didn't do their homework. Spend time conducting thorough research. Information gathering prior to commitment is vital to ensuring mistakes are not made. Don't underestimate the amount of work required before you commit. Be patient, and be prepared to walk away if your research uncovers more negative than positive feedback.

Most successful people work incredibly hard to ensure their success. Don't look at successful people and say, "It must be nice." You may not want to know or do what they've done to get to where they are. Massive success requires massive effort.

Consider buying a franchise rather than freelancing. There are many research tools available to compare franchise opportunities, as opposed to going it alone. Make sure you know the pros and cons ahead of time. Generally, franchises require a larger initial investment. However, even though it's a larger investment, it may minimize your risk exposure. Franchises promise to provide proven methodologies, systems, and cash flow, thus minimizing risk. Consider speaking with franchise owners prior to making any final decisions. I'm not suggesting that franchises are without risk, and I'm not promoting franchises in any way.

Remember also that franchises may offer defined territory. This ensures that no one else opens the same franchise near you.

For example, if you open Bob and Dave's Burgers, a McDonalds could open next to you. If you open your own McDonalds franchise, you've effectively tied up a certain territory. The cost of entry may be high, but the rewards may make it worth it.

Lastly, remember that just because you think a business concept will be successful doesn't mean that it will be. Is there a market for your business? Is there a gap in the market your business could fill? Could your concept be potentially short-lived? Are you prepared for possible future technological advances that could render your concept obsolete?

With the exception of wine and <u>my wife</u>, most things don't get better with age. If you've conducted proper due diligence and the math is not working, consider exploring another opportunity. Don't get lured into thinking that things may change for the better if you simply give it more time. If it doesn't make sense now, it may actually get worse with time and age. Time may compound your debt. Knowing when "to cut bait," as the saying goes, can make or break you. Exiting at the right time, although difficult, can actually save you by allowing you to preserve your credit and/or precious cash. It may be the difference between allowing you to live to invest in another business or going completely broke!

I'm not suggesting that you give up on your dreams. Don't throw in the towel at the first sign of problems. However, if you uncover issues, it's best to get out fast. Use your instincts to your advantage. If it feels wrong and you find yourself having to "shoot from the hip" to decide, it may be best to look elsewhere. Knowing when to cut your losses is a critical part of decision-making. The larger the investment, the more vital knowing when to bail out is.

<u>Get Creative: Other methods to sell when your competition is fierce or has an edge</u>

If all else fails and you can see that, for some reason, you are losing market share to the competition, you have to ask why. You need to research the cause of your loss and take action. For example, your competition has a financing package that allows clients to purchase their product or service with no money down, or they may be offering 0% interest for 12 months. It's your job to match or beat the competition at their own game. Get creative and understand exactly what your buyers want and what's driving their decision to buy your competition's service or product. It may be that your client base is willing to accept an inferior product because of a promotional offer that is too good to pass up.

Remember that selling a more expensive or complex product requires that you effectively explain to and convince your client that your product is the best for them. You can use value analysis to demonstrate that your product may have a higher price, but it <u>costs</u> far less in the long run. It essentially refers to the price as being a one-time higher expense while ownership of an inferior, cheaper product can actually COST a great deal more over time if it breaks or fails. Thus, the product with the best value may be priced higher, but over time, costs far less.

You are not going to get every deal. There will always be clients who you can't sell to regardless of how good your product is. You need to focus on selling to <u>most</u> of your clients. You need to be sure that you have done everything in your power to sell to each and every client before giving up. If the client does nothing or buys from someone else, at least you know that it is not because of your lack of effort. This is essential for being successful in sales. If your competition is going to steal your client and win the deal, be sure you went down with a fight. It is a game; your livelihood is at stake. This game can cost you or make you real money.

Chapter 26

Company Policy for Extending Credit

In a word, don't, unless you have to. I realize that this chapter does not necessarily apply to all salespeople. However, you must get paid in order to consider your product sold. Therefore, I thought it would be relevant to briefly discuss payment. We all want the sale to go through and don't want the payment terms to destroy all of our sales efforts. Obviously, large expensive and/or elaborate products may require significant selling time as well as sales effort. In order to preserve your sale you may choose to enlighten the buyer of your payment terms in advance of receiving your documents. In other words, you probably don't want your buyer to be surprised. If you're able to verbally discuss this, you may be able to soften the perceived harshness of your documents as well as payment terms.

Even with smaller transactions, businesses adopt and implement payment terms. Ever wonder why nearly every restaurant or retail business requires you to pay them before you leave? Because the restaurant or store owner knows that once you leave, the chances of getting paid are slim to none. Whether you pay with a credit card, check, or cash, you know it is a normal procedure. The next reason is that you understand, as the consumer, that it is industry standard to pay prior to exiting the restaurant or retail store. However, what if you're in a business that traditionally doesn't require the clients to pay in advance? What if your client expects 30-day payment terms? What if you're delivering a large, expensive machine, and the client only wants to pay after the machine is delivered? He claims that he's never had to pay in advance from any other company.

You've got some explaining to do. You need to use finesse to persuade your client to pay on your terms. What do I mean by finesse? You need to convince the client that your terms and conditions of payment are industry standard. You can use the old method of stating that it is a company policy. However, it may be best to say something like, "Would you prefer to wire us the funds or use your credit card?" This implies that you expect to be paid without bluntly asking. If the client expects 30-day terms, you can always say that once he establishes credit with you, there should be no problem with 30-day terms. You may also say that it may be best to put the payment on a credit card. That's what credit cards are for. No matter what, try not to lose rapport over your payment policy. Thus, the reason to use tact and finesse.

If the client is pushing back and wants a further explanation as to why they must pay in advance, you can offer several easy-to-swallow reasons. Depending on the client, you may say something like, "The bank doesn't build 'insert your product,' and we don't lend money." It's funny and can be effective. If the client is more serious, you may say, "What are your concerns about paying for this now?" Depending on his response, you can modify accordingly.

You don't want to argue with your client. However, it may be better to discuss this and possibly argue before they get your product. At least you have the upper hand. Once they have the product, they have the upper hand. You need to do everything you can to stay in control of your business. Minimize your exposure to people who may not pay you. You must consider that anyone who you extend credit to may not pay you. Can you handle not being paid by this company or person? If the answer is no, you need to figure out a way to get paid.

Our company applies professional pressure to persuade the client that our payment policy is customary. In business and in life, there are degrees of trust. Some clients may be trusted with $50, while others may be trusted with $5,000. Who you trust and to what degree you trust them are very important. If you extend too much credit to the wrong people, you could get burned. I realize that clients can fill out a credit application, but let the credit card companies handle it if possible. Encourage your clients to pay with cash or pay via wire transfer.

It's better to have no business than to have bad business. Remember to be cautious and create degrees of trust for clients. If you don't have to trust the client, then don't. Even if your company must pay credit card processing fees, it's probably worth it to limit your exposure. I don't want to belabor the point, but you cannot be too cautious. There are reasons we all signed contracts. Think about how many restaurants ask you to sign for purchases less than $100.00. Do they trust you? I don't think so. Yes, they want you to add a tip. However, they are forcing you to sign a legal document that says you will pay the credit card company. Remember to be prudent when it comes to extending credit.

My company deals in big-ticket items for the most part. One out of five clients balk at paying before they receive the machine. It is our job to convince the client that payment in advance is customary and not a big deal. If you absolutely cannot sway the client to pay you before you deliver, you may ask to get a wire transfer upon delivery, preferably prior to unloading.

This adds a layer of insurance and minimizes your risk. Bills of lading can be written to request payment upon delivery. You may want to use a freight carrier that you are familiar with and who knows you do not want your product unloaded until the wire transfer is completed.

You have to be the judge of how far you are willing to go. Your client should be willing to bend a little. If the client is so staunch that they are not flexible at all, you may want to reconsider the deal. Being in business is so much more than just making a product and selling a product. Because you are dealing with people and emotions, it presents many challenges. To consistently succeed, you need to have strategies in place to defer the risks and place you in a power position. You should have the upper hand at all times, especially when it comes to getting paid.

Finale

CEOs, politicians, executives, salespeople, customer service reps, real estate agents, and everyone else who rely on communication to make a living can utilize the tips I've outlined in this book—tips I learned from a lifetime in the business world. Pick and choose the tips that pertain to your particular industry.

No matter what industry you're in, there are universal communication concepts that everyone can utilize. Listen to what people are telling you, regardless of whether or not you agree with them. Work with them even though you feel they are <u>not right</u>. Be patient. When you think your patience has been exhausted, be more patient. Even when pushed, successful people remain calm and collected. Remember, if it were easy, everyone would be successful, and we'd all be the same.

Treat communication as if it were a game. Many games, like poker, require that your opponent does not know what you are thinking. Similarly, the communication game is best played when the other side does not know all of the cards you are holding. It is often best to keep your true feelings, opinions, and thoughts to yourself. Once you've lost your cool, it's like dropping an atom bomb during a war. The negotiations are over. There is no turning back. Lull the other side into submission by never "losing control." Stay the course and be steadfast. Time is a valuable communication weapon.

Another tactic that can save time is to call out the elephant in the room. Mention the elephant and diffuse the concern rapidly. Lastly, if the people you're dealing with "ain't right," you've got to empathize to get what you want. The best of the best will implement these communication concepts and strategies. In the end, you'll not only save time, but you'll also get what you want much faster.

How do you stay focused and inspired? We've all heard the cliché to learn from the most successful people and emulate their success. However, it's hard to relate to the top ten most successful people in the world. You may aspire to become a billionaire but can't relate to a billionaire at this point. To get a dose of reality that is still inspiring but more realistic, read the LinkedIn bios of local business leaders, lawyers, doctors, preachers, etc. You'll be astonished by their achievements. It is incredible to view all of the bios and see where all of the people have been in their lives. The schools they have attended, the countries they have visited, the awards they have earned will be an eye-opener. These successful but not necessarily famous people should be a source of inspiration for you.

Let's face it, there are millions of people who want to be successful. We all know that many factors determine what constitutes success. Most people will settle for or aspire to be better than average. The harsh reality is that you may be in competition with the very people you aspire to be like. You may be competing with people you graduated with. Make no mistake—life has winners and losers and people who are on the bench. To be a winner, you will face tough competitors. Your competitor may be another advertiser, service provider, or machine salesman. Your competitor could be a doctor or lawyer who is bidding on the house you want to buy.

In life and in general, you need to understand that the world is full of people who want what you want. I'm not saying you need to compare yourself to others. You can use comparisons to gauge your success level on your terms. Be true to yourself. <u>You only need to impress yourself.</u> Don't live to impress or get the approval or praise of others. I look to impress God and myself. I want my family to be proud of me, but I am not looking to impress them.

In the end, we can't take anything with us. We can leave an inspirational legacy behind. That is what you must strive for in sales, life, and business. Be the best that <u>YOU</u> can be. Pay attention to others and view their achievements as inspiration for yourself. You're going to look around—just don't be jealous of others. Be happy for everyone and do your best. After all, you want others to be happy for you. You want others to pull for you. God will bless you when you treat others the way that you want to be treated.

Remember, people don't plan to fail; people fail to plan! You must plan to be successful. You must plan to continue to learn each day. You must plan to take educated risks. You must plan to better yourself and those around you. You must plan to make a difference in this world. You must plan and strive for peace of mind by knowing you have done everything in your power to be the best person that you can be.

You've got nothing to lose by trying to improve yourself. Life is a learning journey. The sales techniques and advice in this book may help you in countless ways, some of which may have nothing to do with sales. You may take away some advice that helps you negotiate an excessive auto repair bill. You may gain knowledge that helps you at a job interview. No matter what, there is probably something here that will help you. It's up to you to find the gold and see if it can be made into a ring that fits your finger!

Remember to be FAITHFUL and THANKFUL! Stay focused on achieving your dreams and goals, and at the same time, don't neglect the people who love and rely on you. Responsible people are never selfish and always put their loved ones first. Remember, you're lucky if you get 100 years to do it all. Balance your time wisely. Find a happy medium. All work and no play is foolish. Rather, I suggest adopting the old adage, "Work hard and play hard."

Take the time to appreciate the good times. The good times, "the reprieve," may be short-lived. Enjoy it while it lasts. Treat your problems as if they were challenges. Don't take yourself or life too seriously. Your goal is to win the game of LIFE! Good luck. All the best.

The End.

Y'all Ain't Right "Funnies"

LET ME GIVE YOU SOME funny examples of why I classify some clients as "not right." I was giving directions to a client several years ago. The client's starting point was almost exactly five miles east of us. As there are no direct routes from his current location to ours, I gave him the option of going north for five miles and then heading south another seven miles. The other option I gave him was to go south for five miles and then head north another seven miles. His response, in his southern accent, was, "You almost have to start from someplace else to get there."

About 10 years ago, we had scheduled a training session for maintenance employees. We invited them to visit our location so that we could conduct live training at the factory. The training was scheduled to start at 10 am. One of our best clients requested that we wait for his people to arrive. They were approximately two hours away by car. They left at 8 am, so we assumed they would be on time. At 10:30 am, we hadn't heard from or seen them. We called our client to see if he had heard from them, but he had not heard anything. We continued to wait—11 o'clock, 12 o'clock, 1 o'clock, and still no word from the maintenance guys.

Finally, at 1:45 pm, they arrived at our location. Our client was furious, we were frustrated, and the training guys looked dumbfounded. We were all looking for an explanation as to why they were so late and were surprised that they were not spouting off what happened to them or why they were so late. We thought they would have an incredible story to tell.

Clearly, they were not planning on providing an explanation. We finally said, "Where have you guys been? We've been waiting for you since 10 am. Why didn't you let someone know where you were? Why didn't you call?" They responded casually, "We were 'bout to." That's southern for, "I don't understand what all the fuss is about." They had no valid reason and no explanation at all. To this day, nobody knows exactly where those two boys were for nearly six hours.

We were interviewing candidates for a Welder/Fabricator position in the factory—a tough job that requires both strength and welding skills. After several interviews, we chose one man with a southern drawl. We started to explain the job in more detail. He stood, eyes glazed over, as we showed him blueprints, sketches, and assembly drawings. After about 10 minutes describing in detail what the position entails, the future employee said, "I'll do whatever you tell me to do. However, when you hire me, you hire me from the neck, down." In other words, the brain does not come with the employee. We hired him on the spot. You gotta appreciate his candor.

Another employee, Tom, had worked at a large union mill for many years. After the mill closed, we hired him. Let's just say, he brought his "mill" work ethic and "union" ways to our business. I'm not bashing mills or unions, but they do not share our work practices. We may be a little harder on our employees. We expect them to work hard and fast. One day, Tom was taking several breaks and smoking cigarettes while working.

Another employee yelled over to Tom and said, "Hey Tom, you need to get a little pep in your step!" Tom exclaimed, "I got TWO speeds. If you don't like this one, you definitely won't like the next one!"

"Hey, Scott?" one employee yelled to another. Scott says, "Yeah?" You look a lot better goin' than you do comin'!

We hired the local volunteer fire chief who also suffered from a stutter. One day, he was over four hours late to work. We confronted him and asked why he was late. What was his excuse for not calling? He said his house caught on fire and bbbbburnt to the gggground. He was discharged as fire chief shortly thereafter.

We had a client leave a message on Sunday. His message said, "They've got our plane, they've got our plane! I'm not buying anything now. We're going to war!" He was referring to the incident that occurred several years ago when the Chinese government detained one of our downed military planes. In essence, they would not release our plane. We all felt they were keeping it to copy our technology. It wasn't an invasion. However, our client "freaked out" over it. The point is that he was willing to postpone or cancel a purchase because he believed we might go to war. It was certainly a stretch of the imagination. Like I said, "Y'ALL AINT RIGHT!

About the Author

Why Should You Listen to Me?

First... Why should you listen to me? Maybe you shouldn't. Why read anything I have written? Who the heck am I to give advice? I believe that you should definitely question the source of the advice you are being given, even if it is me. One of the biggest mistakes people make is to listen to the wrong people. Advice is like food. Eat the wrong food, and you'll get sick.

I am a self-proclaimed sales expert. I have no degree. I have no awards or trophies for sales. I'm not much different from all of the other self-proclaimed gurus. I'll let you be the judge of if what I've written has any substance. I've become a well-rounded sales professional through experience. I've read dozens of books, plus I've listened to and have watched hundreds of videos. In other words, my experience and success has been learned and taught to me by others, in addition to being hands on. I've tried to take at least one valuable lesson or word of advice from each and every book or video I've read or watched. I believe there is gold somewhere in nearly every book. You may even find a hidden golden nugget in this book.

My father owned and operated rock quarries, sand and gravel mines, and concrete companies. I worked for him during high school and college. Now, we are partners in manufacturing and distribution. In short, I have years of hands-on experience selling a technical, highly specialized product globally. I have sold millions of dollars worth of machinery. I have sold thousands of machines to individuals, corporations, and the US military. I have numerous patents and trademarks in a variety of countries. I started from the ground up as a laborer, mechanic, and operator in the mining industry. I literally touched, smelled, and experienced the industry I have spent my life in.

There is no better way to become an authority in your trade or industry than to experience each and every aspect of it. Some things can't be read in a book; you have to actually go out and experience it for yourself. Having said that, I don't believe that every car salesman should have to work at an auto assembly plant or become a mechanic. However, the more you know about your industry and product, the easier and more successful your sales career will be. You've just learned a gem about sales. Become an authority on your product, and your buyer will listen to your advice, even if it causes them pain.

Selling isn't just about selling products for a commission or for financial gain. Selling may be persuading your children to go to college. Selling is communication on steroids. Can you communicate at a level to be a great salesperson? Charisma, personality, tonality, the message itself, the product, and each and every aspect of how you conduct yourself while interacting with others is important. What resonates with kids, spouses, and customers is that when all is said and done, your motivation is to HELP them. Sales are about helping the buyer to see how your product will benefit them.

I cannot take credit for all of the content contained herein. My mother and father played a huge part in shaping who I am. My wife, daughter, son, family, and friends also contributed to my development. Many advisors, teachers, authors, and public speakers have also contributed to making my ideologies more well-rounded. We are all the products of our environment.

I would like to pay tribute and give credit to the following people: Zig Ziglar, Brian Tracy, Tom Hopkins, my psychology and communication professors, Jesus, Billy Graham, Joel Osteen, Chris Voss, Ben Franklin, Grant Cardone, Stuart Diamond, Jordan Belfort, Ronald Reagan, special needs individuals and families, Jack Lemon, and John Wayne—to name a few of the most influential and inspirational. I have gained something from each one of these organizations and people. I have been affected, influenced, and inspired by the bravery, determination, and fortitude of those who are less fortunate, handicapped, disabled, or in despair. I'm blown away by those who demonstrate character, kindness, and happiness on a consistent basis. I'm inspired by the less fortunate, who don't allow negativity, to guide their lives.

I believe in being patriotic and never forgetting the brave men and women who gave their lives or have been wounded in defense of our freedoms. Understand that our nation, as a whole, is bigger than any one of our personal opinions or agendas. We are one United States with millions of people, all different yet similar in our belief that freedom gives us the platform to speak our mind. It is this freedom that allows us to express ourselves openly and without condemnation.

And it is our freedom that allows us to be tolerant of others who staunchly disagree with us. Millions have paid the price for this precious freedom. I believe in never being so egotistical as to believe that my message is worth disgracing the brave people who have fought to uphold those truths that we so frequently take for granted. I believe in standing during our National Anthem while saluting and honoring our flag. I believe in respecting the office of the President, regardless of their party. I believe that restraint and respect will always be more effective than foul language and shocking behavior. I believe in demonstrating humility and being kind to everyone. One should always be humble, courteous, faithful, and appreciative. One should try to stay positive and remember to smile and laugh often.

I feel incredibly blessed and extremely fortunate to have been given the opportunities that I have been given. I've combined opportunity and hard work in an effort to make a difference while maintaining my standards. I strive for success and never sacrifice my ethics or integrity. It's not always easy, and I'm still learning ways to handle different situations respectfully. At 50 years of age, I felt compelled to share my experiences and insights in the hope that someone may derive something from it. I wanted to create a reference guide/book by sharing my accumulated hands-on knowledge gained through hard-earned" experiences.

It is my sincere hope and prayer that some of what I have written will be beneficial to both young and old. We live in the information age. Everything is accessible to all who take advantage of it. Life will be hard—yes, that's true. Why not keep an open mind and continue to gain wisdom from your predecessors? The journey will be far easier if you apply the knowledge you accumulate and make an effort to become a better person.

LIVING LIFE

Life is not a race, but indeed a journey. Be honest. Work hard. Be choosy.

Say "Thank you," "I love you," and "Great job" to someone each day. Go to church, take time for prayer. The Lord giveth and the Lord taketh. Let your handshake mean more than pen and paper.

Love your life and what you've been given. It is not accidental. Search for your purpose and do it the best that you can. Dreaming does matter. It allows you to become that which you aspire to be.

Laugh often. Appreciate the little things in life, and enjoy them. Some of the best things in life really are free.

Do not worry; less wrinkles are more becoming. Forgive, it frees the soul. Take time for yourself. Plan for longevity. Recognize the special people you've been blessed to know.

Live for today, enjoy the moment.

—Bonnie L. Mohr

www.ingramcontent.com/pod-product-compliance
Lightning Source LLC
Chambersburg PA
CBHW072029230526
45466CB00020B/1183